Ancient Wisdom

Invoking the Power
of
Your Soul Star

Richard Dupuis
with Carol Skakel

Aurum Publishing Company
Lynnwood, Washington

Library of Congress Catalog Card Number 95-77285

ISBN 0-9646654-0-9

Aurum Publishing Company
P. O. Box 2308
Lynnwood, Washington 98036
(206) 774-9760

Cover painting:
"A Master of the Wisdom"
© 1994 Carmen Murray

First edition July 1995
Manufactured in the United States of America

Contents

Acknowledgments

I wish to gratefully acknowledge and thank the many individuals, guides and Masters who have helped me to bring this book to fruition.

Thank you, Sanaya Roman and Duane Packer, for teaching me how to channel and receive the inspiration of Spirit, and for bringing the Light Body teachings into this dimension.

Thank you, Carol Skakel. As my co-writer, editor and confidante, you made this book possible, and you probably put more work into it than I did.

Thank you, Richard Krull, for being the co-author for my first book, *Creating Your Light Body,* and for teaching me the abc's of authorship.

Thank you, Karin Elofson, for your friendship and support in so many ways during the writing of this book.

Thank you, Carmen Murray, for the beautiful cover artwork of a Master of the Wisdom.

A special thank you to Dr. David L. Clarke, my former psychoanalyst. David, you were the first person ever to talk to me in this lifetime about Spirit. You opened up a whole new world to me and you helped me to find meaning and purpose in my life.

Lastly, I would like to thank Kirk Gardner and Aurum Publishing for the final editing and production of the book.

Preface

A Message from Vywamus:

In the pages of this book you will find much ancient wisdom translated into modern form. This knowledge was first given to the ancient Masters in Lemuria and Atlantis. It is understood by the Hierarchy in charge of this planet that you seek to let go of the shackles of this reality and bring more Light and Love into your life.

The ancients and even some of your more modern Masters had to sacrifice much of their lives in order to reach enLightenment, and many have given up decades of their time for its rewards. Those of us in charge of shepherding your planet through these times of change are now offering an alternative. We are losing patience, so to speak, with the slow pace of the evolution of humanity. (Of course we never really become impatient because it is inevitable that you will choose Light and Love if not in this lifetime in another).

That still creates a dilemma for us now, however, because there is a time frame for humanity to move into the fourth dimension. You are in that time now and the window is open to the masses, but they are slow to comprehend it.

We have encouraged Richard and Carol to write down these teachings and produce this book. Many thousands of years ago they were given a similar task: to give form to what were then the ancient teachings that became the Old Testament. Because of their success they have been given a new task: to make contemporary another ancient teaching.

When they received these teachings they had no idea how significant they would be both for themselves and for others. At the time they were given the teachings they received only the basics. Of course they wanted the whole nine yards, so to speak, but because we wanted them to develop the ideas along contemporary lines we gave only the basics, knowing that their enthusiasm, curiosity, and desire to evolve and heal their lives would ensure the development of this work.

They have succeeded grandly in producing the very simple but powerful teachings herein. To say the least, we are pleased.

April 20th, 1994
VYWAMUS
Guardian of the Light for this Cosmic Day

Introduction

Vywamus is a channeled entity who has been given the task by the Source of our Universe to bring new teachings and new information to the Earth.

The teachings in this book are ancient but contemporized to fit a modern culture. Except for the information in the chapter on Creating Your Light Body they are new to our Universe.

In fact the energy of the Tenth Ray, the Light Body ray, only anchored on this planet a few months ago. New or ancient, we believe that the simple, powerful techniques given in this book will accelerate your growth beyond anything you could have imagined.

As stated by Vywamus in the introduction, we write about ancient techniques with a very modern and contemporary base. We have updated these techniques to the point where the ancients would probably not even recognize them. We are satisfied that we have refined them to the point where they are a quantum leap ahead of what the old Masters taught.

These techniques (which we teach in our week-end workshops) have enabled participants to take on as much growth in one weekend as would ordinarily have taken them two years or more. We are aware, of course, that we are not alone in developing new techniques for facilitating growth. From all corners of the Earth new wisdom is coming forth. This is as it should be.

For those with a strong desire to grow, heal and become bearers of Light and Love for themselves and the planet, there is a great deal of help in the form of physical teachers and others from the Spirit Realms such as Vywamus.

In the past, those who reached enLightenment, who achieved the status of Master, dedicated their entire lives toward the attainment of their goal. With the teachings in this book you can achieve the same result in a few half hours each week, meditating and using the Soul Star Mantra, and the invocations that we recommend. Should you wish to accelerate your transformation even more, you can learn to activate your Light Body.

Bringing your Light Body into this dimension is the most significant step you can take in your Spiritual growth and evolution. No other step or process is more growth enhancing. Your Light Body is your Christ consciousness. Becoming a living Christ is your destiny, whether you know it or not. You can do so in this lifetime if you choose to, or in another if you are not ready now. The choice is yours.

The tools are available in this book to transform your emotional body, release your fear and anger, and work with your other issues. Using the techniques we recommend you will quickly expand and raise your consciousness. Those are indeed the steps and processses to enLightenment and Ascension.

Ascension is a much talked about and greatly misunderstood event (in fact, it is not really an event, but a process). Physical Ascension has never been achieved on this planet. All Ascensions have been Ascensions of the etheric body and other energies, like those of the aura and consciousness. The authors are rapidly evolving towards their own physical Ascension. They may not be the first to do so, but they believe physical Ascension is inevitable for themselves or indeed for anyone who chooses to make use of the tools and techniques described in this book.

Not only are there tools and techniques to help you to grow, but there are procedures for connecting with and calling on your guides to assist you with your growth.

We also provide you with ways to clear and harmonize your emotional body and release old stuck beliefs that limit you in your everyday life. This is extremely important because if you hold beliefs that are contrary to what you are trying to accomplish, you simply cannot achieve the growth you desire.

Old beliefs must be released if you are to move forward. Working with your higher energies, your Soul and your Light Body, will automatically bring those limiting beliefs into your awareness so that you can release them.

You may call on the authors or those from the other side of the veils to help you with your growth; either way you will not be disappointed. Whether you are just beginning in your exploration of Metaphysics or have been interested in these matters for many years, you will find something in the pages of this book that will have a profound impact on your growth.

We wish you the greatest success on your journey and we stand ready to serve you in whatever way we can,

Richard Dupuis and Carol Skakel

Chapter One   Ancient Wisdom

A Message from Sanat Kumara:

I am the Ancient of Days, Sanat Kumara, Head of the Council of Light for this quadrant of the Universe.

Eons ago the Council of Light decided this quadrant of the Universe and especially this emerald green planet called Earth was to be populated. However, at that time the Earth was not quite as beautiful as it is now. The beauty of this planet is partly the result of biological experimentation and partly the result of mutations that occurred more than thirty million years ago when the planet was under the control of the dynoids.

The dynoids were a race of reptilian like beings that had conquered the human population on Earth. The human population then was very unlike the humans who are here today, however they were of the Adam Kadmon lineage that is dispersed throughout this Universe and fifty two others.

The Kadmons have two arms, two legs, a torso and head. The Adam Kadmon were the creation of the being called Metatron and other genetic engineers who worked with him to create humans and other biological beings. Metatron is the Archangel who is closest to the Source.

Because of the ongoing difficulties on this planet - wars, destruction and complete annihilation of various peoples and races during the last thirty five million years, the High Council on Sirius sent me and two other humans to Earth some eighteen million years ago to help stabilize the populace of this grand planet.

You have free will here, so there is only so much we could do then or now. Your fate is and always has been in your hands. But along with your free will you have also been given the co creating power of the Gods. For most of your history you have not used this great power appropriately. Instead of creating love, peace, prosperity and abundance for all, you have played the game of power and control over others. You have conquered and been conquered during the history of this Universe and this planet.

We speak about all of you who have the Adam Kadmon lineage and who have free will, not just those of you on this planet alone.

You are a restless bunch, you Kadmons, you have great power to create, to love and even to make war, and you have done so for your entire history in spite of many admonishments from the Spirit Councils who shepherd this Universe. Entire planets have been destroyed as a result of your mischief. Civilizations have been entirely wiped out, so many that they are countless in number.

Your true history is of course very much unknown to you because you have been lied to and controlled and even mutated from your original design and capabilities. Did you know that at one time you had multidimensional capabilities and awareness? That is now gone, yet you still have much, if not all of the potential that you brought with you from the star systems that provided the seeding of the human race.

You were indeed born upon the seas, but not in the way your scientists now believe. You did not evolve from a single celled amoeba or anything like it. You were of all conscious, sentient, intelligent beings right from the beginning. In fact, much more conscious than you are now. You have the capacity to return to full consciousness now.

What is full consciousness? Full consciousness is awareness of who you are. Your multidimensionality, your so-called past lives (all lives are now), and even your future lives.

An awareness of the history of the planet and your history on other planets is held within your DNA. You are a living library of information. Deep within your cellular structure and your bone marrow are ancient memories of long forgotten civilizations that have come and gone. Also there are memories of your own role on this planet and others, all your history is contained in the library you carry with you from the time you burst forth and separated from your Source until now.

With full consciousness you will remember who you are, why and how you got here and what your assignment is. The Source gave all of you an assignment when you individualized, but it has long been forgotten. Every lifetime is part of that assignment no matter how small or insignificant it may appear. That is why you have been provided with the information, so that when you finally go home that information can be decoded by the Source.

You have felt alone and unloved much of the time on this journey because that was also part of your contract with Source, to explore separateness and individuality of experience.

You have done marvelously well with your assignments, you carry millions of bits of information in your cells and your DNA. You are being called home now but home is not someplace else; it is where you are, it is the soil beneath your feet. The Earth is your adopted home and you can experience the journey home without ever leaving it.

You probably aren't aware of it, but this shining emerald green planet is the focus of the entire Galaxy at this time for a number of reasons. You who read this are the chosen ones, you are the Light Bearers for all of humanity. You have come here as members of the Council of Light for this quadrant of the Universe. You have gathered here from all over the Galaxy, from remote planets and star systems too many to count to the port of the return of the planet to its rightful place as a beacon of Love and Light for all to see and emulate.

You are here on the most urgent of assignments, most of you were seeded here centuries ago and have been walking this plane of existence wondering why you were here and what it is all about. You have felt this unquenchable thirst to know why you were here, why you seemed so stranded and abandoned in a place with so much pain and suffering.

On a Cosmic scale it has only been moments, but to you every lifetime seems eternal, when you are struggling from day to day to survive. Well, the news is this. I am Sanat Kumara, your Planetary Governor on the Spiritual plane, and I tell you who read this, your Light has been switched on. We, the Keepers of Time of the solar script for humanity and Earth have thrown the switch, you have been unlocked, you need not struggle to survive or live in misery or poverty. You can move ahead in unprecedented ways, you can shed the burdens of hundreds even thousands of past lives in months, maybe even less time than that. We are supplying you with these keys and there will be others.

We have thrown the switch and opened a doorway for you that was formerly closed and locked. There is an ancient coding deep within your cellular structure and your DNA that kept you from activating your full consciousness and potential. That is no longer true, we have unlocked the coding that has kept the members of the Council of Light from knowing who they are. You have done your homework, you have graduated and it is time for you to quickly shed your karma and your limitations and claim your place as a full member of the Council of Light.

The Earth is under the stewardship of the Council and is a full member of the Council of Light. Its coding has also been unlocked and the consciousness which is the planet is accelerating, you call this Ascension. Your planet is ascending, changing dimensions, it has taken its cue and is progressing into the fourth dimension from the third, where it currently resides. Actually it has very recently moved into the first division of the fourth dimension. This should signal a warning to all of you because very few of you are in alignment with this shift from one dimension to the other.

In the past when a planet moved from one dimension to another there were only small pockets of survivors, and that could happen again; however, we expect enough of you will awaken to avert this kind of catastrophe in your future. It need not occur, we have done our part by unlocking your coding and "jump starting" if you will, your awakening.

Even those of you who do not feel that you are already members of the Council of Light can become members. There are steps you can take to gain full membership. Begin by asking the Universe to hear you and bring you the necessary information and experiences to qualify you for full membership. Ask and ye shall receive.

All of you need to begin clearing your emotional body of your fears, anger and outmoded beliefs and other false programming. The Earth has begun its own clearing and you must also if you are to be part of the evolution of your planet. You are an integral part of the Earth's ecosystem, you are not separate. You are as much a part of the Earth as the trees, the rocks and streams and the animals. You are absolutely necessary to the health of the Earth. You and it share consciousness, you are of its energies.

The vibrations of the planet are rising even faster than that of humanity. The discrepancy is not so great that it cannot be corrected, you still have enough time to catch up. If enough of you choose to awaken, all is not lost, but it will take millions of you, enough to create a critical mass for humanity to awaken as a whole.

You play an important role, those of you willing to come forward at this time. You must raise your vibrations to match those of the planet. This is not a difficult task, you can do it as suggested by this book or in similar ways you find elsewhere. Remember we have unlocked your coding for you, you are no longer restricted in any way from reaching those higher states of consciousness that are called enLightenment by many, but you must take action. Your future is up to you.

Chapter Two   Cause and Effect

A Message from Sanat Kumara:

I am the Ancient of Days, Sanat Kumara, and I have come to bring you this grand message. You no longer need to be a slave to your karma, you can release it all at once.

You have carried your karmic template throughout all of your lifetimes. It has varied in shape, in color, in density from time to time, but it has always been with you, it is one of the few absolutes you experience on this dimension.

Your karma has provided your lesson, shaped your experience and created your limitations. I know you have been told by your many new age prophets that you are unlimited and that is true; without karma you can become unlimited.

Your Soul of course, knows no limitations, when unrestricted by karma and physical form. Your vibratory frequencies also create some restrictions for you; the higher the frequencies, the greater the awareness and the less restriction you experience.

You have come to play with these limitations and restrictions, to learn about and experience them. Most of you have done an excellent job of learning to be limited, but now you can begin to release those restrictions like never before. Help is amassing all over your planet. Teachers are appearing to you in Spirit and in physical form. At your command are legions of Masters and·Angels and even Archangels to work with you and guide you. With their help there is nothing you cannot accomplish.

Karma is released as you walk through your lessons, as you learn and increase your understanding of your fear, your anger and your beliefs. Your beliefs are made possible and molded by your karma as well. Your beliefs of course are your reality. They are what is reflected back to you along with your fear and your anger in your relationships. Releasing your karma will allow you to release all of your fear, all of your anger and false beliefs.

Without karma you will be able to take on the higher energies like those of your Soul Star and your Light Body with ease.

Without Karma you will be able to let go of your addictive relationships and break your ties with that old karmic group that you have incarnated with for all of the eons you have walked this plane. They will no longer hold you in their limited embrace. For some of you of course, breaking those old ties will create feelings of loss. You always have the choice, to stay with whoever you want to. And if you choose to stay with someone from that group, you can, but you will find it increasingly difficult to share space with those whose vibration does not match yours. They can of course release their karma and raise their vibrations just like you have.

Kryon

Richard Dupuis: "I first met and began to channel Kryon after reading one of two books Kryon has channeled through Lee Carroll. Kryon is a Master in service to humanity and is in charge of retuning the gridwork of this planet so that it can ascend into the fourth dimension. Without this realignment the Earth would not have survived."

A Message from Kryon:

The Ancient One, Sanat Kumara, has given me permission to speak to you about this great new power of yours. It was with his grace and wisdom that we have been able to bring this new gift to you.

Releasing your karma has become very simple through the advent of this new plan for you and your planet. All you have to do in your meditations or out loud while sitting quietly, before you go to bed, request of your guides that they lift your karma, your karmic template or implant. They will do so if you are ready.

You are ready if you are able to control your ego's compulsiveness. If you understand how your ego tries to control your reality and if you can separate your ego's consistent demands for control over your life.

This means you must have the ability to stop listening to ego and listen instead to the wisdom of your Soul. You will have a stronger connection to your Soul once you have released your karma. You currently have a karmic implant that separates you from your own Soul so that you can experience the duality of this time and place. This is not a penalty. You have chosen this as your way of experiencing this reality.

Now it is time for you to choose to live your life differently. To release this restriction so you can experience your entire Soul essence on this dimension. It is actually imperative that you release your Soul for this event. Asking your guides to lift your karma will trigger some events you must know about before making that decision.

First, there are two guides who have been with you since birth, these are not guides you have been aware of. No matter how attuned and connected to the Masters and guides you might be, these guides have remained intentionally obscure to you, that is their way.

During the period of time you are releasing your karmic templates, approximately ninety days for most, these guides will leave. That will create deep feelings of loss for you and your Soul and it will continue during the ninety days, some will feel this more than others. You may also experience some feelings of depression, abandonment and other emotional states, but they will not be unbearable and you will easily survive them. This will vary from individual to individual and will not last beyond the ninety days.

At the end of that period more advanced guides will take their place and you will have three instead of two. These guides will be able to communicate more easily with you. You will have a verbal connection to them.

Without your karma you will not be connected to the events that your karma would automatically connect you with. You will have a clean slate so to speak. You will want to make new contacts with those three new guides that are with you after you release your karma. You decide for yourself how your life should look and then you ask them to make it look that way.

You see, all of you had certain karmic connections that made up your goal imprints, for better or worse. You will no longer have those imprints.

The advantage is that you have released those negative connections, but you may have released the positive ones as well. That will not be a problem for you, simply ask your new guides to reconnect you with the desirable goals that were part of your old karmic pattern. Or create for yourself a new plan or simply ask your guides to create a positive new future for you, one of love, joy and abundance.

Without your karmic restrictions you will find new shifts, new growth and change come much more quickly. You will be able to take on new higher frequencies of Light more readily and release old beliefs, fears and anger more easily. Many of the old programs will simply go with your old karmic imprint, and they will no longer affect you.

This is very new. Never before in your history have you been able to release your karma this way. It is a gift from those of us in service who work with your Planetary Hierarchy.

Richard: "Releasing my karma this way has created many new changes for me, some addictive behaviors are completely gone. Growth comes much more easily and my psychic and intuitive faculties have improved. Some karmic entanglements have simply vanished.

I have asked for a new contract to get my work out and be more involved in assisting others to develop their Spirituality.

I have been given a new assignment and mission by the Masters and I can see that the work is more exciting than I ever expected.

I recommend that you read the books by Kryon before asking for your karma to be lifted so that you have a clear understanding of what the process is all about. The ninety day period can be intense and difficult, but the time passes quickly and for most it is not an unduly difficult time. After the first few weeks most are hardly aware that they are still in the process. You will not build new karma after releasing the old karma, it is no longer part of our experience on this planet.

Those of you willing and ready to take this step and the others we have written about will experience physical and Spiritual renewal. Your life will change and you will begin to reap the rewards available to all who choose to step into the Light and reclaim their heritage as members of the Council of Light."

Chapter Three   The Soul Star

A Message from Sananda:

As you activate your Soul Star you begin to bring into this reality that which you call your Christ Consciousness. You will learn how to activate your Soul Star in the following chapter. It is important for you to know that each of you have within your energy capsule the energies of a living Christ. As your energies unfold and you evolve towards enLightenment you begin to activate and call on that Christed energy.

You have all been here, on this planet, many times and each time you have gained more knowledge and information about who you are. But you have become lost in the density of this the third dimension. Now you have a chance to take part in the greatest experiment ever performed on this planet. Its Ascension.

As you have walked this plane for the eons of time you have been here, you have yet to discover while being incarnate who you really are. Being on this planet is synonymous with forgetting who you are, so that you can experience a reawakening. In a sense you have come here to play with your reflection. Your reflection is like your shadow, always with you, but like your shadow in the noonday sun it cannot always be seen.

One day in the not too distant future you will come around a corner in what you call your existence and your life; when you do that you will come to see your reflection, the face of your own Soul. The face of your

Soul being reflected back to you will change you for-ever on this planet. You will be healed by that reflec-tion. You will be charmed by it. You will begin to ex-perience love, joy, peace and harmony. You will be seeing your own reflection upon the still waters of your Soul's Light.

As you come face to face with the countenance of your reflection you will begin to activate all of your higher energies including your Soul Star, your Light Body and your Christ Light . Your Soul Star, your Light Body and your higher self are all aspects of your own Christ Consciousness. Your own energy capsule con-tains all of that consciousness and energy that you define as Christ Consciousness. You have just to acti-vate them. You can begin to do so by playing with your Soul Star, learning to invoke higher energies and creating a dialogue with your Soul and higher self.

You are every bit as magnificent as all of the Masters, Saints and guides whom you so venerate. By venerating your own Light and wisdom you begin your journey back home to the higher dimensions and planes of Love . All this by coming face to face with your own reflection, your Soul.

In all of the literature now available to those on a Spiritual path, the Soul Star is rarely mentioned, except in the most eso-teric writings. Even then it is mentioned only briefly, yet it is one of the most powerful energy systems that you possess.

The Soul Star and its powers of transformation have had little recognition so far even within the metaphysical community. Why this should be is anyone's guess. Perhaps in our culture things have to appear complex and difficult before they are deemed important, or perhaps the time has just not been right. Now that the planet as a whole is experiencing the influx of higher energies leading people to an ever greater awareness of their Spiritual nature, the time is ripe for this important information to be made available.

Activating your Soul Star is an incredibly simple and yet amazingly effective way of transforming your energies and reaching higher states of consciousness.

Your Soul Star contains the multidimensional energies of your Soul. Each time it is activated, it infuses more of Soul's Light into your body and energy systems. Bringing more of your Soul's energy and Light into your everyday life and into your energies is one of the most powerful transformational experiences you can have.

Transformation is about awakening your connection to your Soul and its energies. This, of course, is also the way of Ascension, which we will discuss later in the book.

Your Soul Star is your physical connection to your Soul's energy and Light. It is a sphere or ball of energy about six inches above your head and is about six to eight inches in diameter. The energy of your Soul Star can, with continued activation, transform your physical energies and begin to build and activate your Light Body. No other physical energy system is capable of doing this as quickly and efficiently as your Soul Star.

Activating your Soul Star is an important transformational process and for those who wish to evolve in this lifetime, its importance cannot be overstated.

When you infuse your energies and your DNA with your Soul's Light, you are beginning to transform your body at its deepest levels. Your DNA will respond to your Soul's energy by developing new strands and helices of DNA. Ultimately you will develop twelve DNA strands and complete your body's transformation to a much higher state.

One way to transform your DNA and to begin to develop a

DNA with twelve strands is to simply hold your DNA in your awareness and repeat the Soul Star Mantra below. This will actually start the growth of a much more complex DNA, one capable of transforming and ascending the physical body.

The Soul Star is activated by a mantra that invokes the power of the Soul itself. This mantra was first given to Alice Bailey, who channeled twenty or so books with her spirit guide, Djwal Khul, in the first half of this century. It was simplified by the authors of <u>The Rainbow Bridge</u> who refer to themselves as The Two Disciples, and use no other names. <u>The Rainbow Bridge</u> is now somewhat outdated, but nonetheless it is a very good book about the Soul Star.

This is the Soul Star Mantra:

I AM THE SOUL
I AM THE LIGHT DIVINE
I AM LOVE
I AM WILL
I AM FIXED DESIGN

This is a mantra, not an affirmation. It activates your Soul Star and floods your physical and etheric energies with your Soul's energy and Light. The result is that each time you recite the mantra, you are ***permanently raising your vibrations to a higher frequency.***

The energy of your Soul Star is so powerful that you could probably reach enLightenment and Ascension by doing nothing more than meditating on the Mantra. You could very well reach the third level of Initiation, the Soul merge, by doing the mantra alone. The Soul merge or third level of Initiation is the point where the Soul comes down from the Soul Star and actually anchors in the thymus gland just above your heart. This is considered to be the first major Initiation and is overseen by Sanat

Kumara, the embodiment of the Earth Soul. From this point on, you are Soul-directed to a large extent, whether you know it or not.

This is the step that we all must make if we are to align with the ascension of the planet. When enough people have taken this step humanity will begin to look very different and we will see significant changes in our institutions and political structures. We have developed many techniques and ways of using the mantra that greatly enhance its effectiveness so that you can accelerate your growth processes.

When you ignite your Soul Star by reciting the Mantra, the energy pulses downwards along the antahkarana. The antahkarana is a cord of Light and energy that runs along your spinal column into the Earth and connects you with the planetary energies. It also goes upwards, through your Soul Star, and connects you with higher cosmic energies.

The development of the antahkarana is so important that without it you cannot reach those high states of consciousness and awareness that indicate your readiness for higher levels of consciousness or Initiation. The antahkarana is a channel for Light and the higher energies. The Soul Star and the antahkarana are very important in the transformation of your energies to fifth dimensional frequencies.

Those of you who are clairvoyant will be able to see the activation of the Soul Star when you focus your attention on it. As you work with the Soul Star and the Mantra, you will begin to feel and experience the intensity of this energy. You can enhance the development of the antahkarana through your imagination, by holding it in your awareness as you do the Mantra. This step is particularly important when you first begin to use the Soul Star Mantra. The Rainbow Bridge, or antahkarana, enables you to bring the highest energies of the Source into your own personal energy field for greater transformation.

Discovering your life purpose - that is, your Soul's intent and desire for this lifetime, can be very important to your growth. Most of you will recognize the meaning of the phrases that make up the Mantra, except for the last phrase, I AM FIXED DESIGN. Encoded in the energies of your fixed design are the skills you can develop, your aptitudes, and the paths you can follow that are in alignment with your purpose. The reason your Soul incarnated at this time and the main lesson your Soul wanted to learn or accomplish during this incarnation are also encoded in these energies. The phrase "life purpose" refers to your major lesson in this lifetime rather than the work or job that you do, though it may be this also. Often people work at jobs or live their lives without being in alignment with their Soul's purpose, and thus they live a frustrating and unfulfilled existence. When we are in tune with our Soul's purpose we are in harmony with the Universe, and life flows more easily for us.

A life purpose can be almost anything. Many people who are incarnate today have a general purpose such as healing this lifetime. When that is the case they will more than likely feel fulfilled by working in the healing arts. You could also fulfill your life purpose by being a gardener, a musician, a teacher, a parent, or almost anything else. Life purposes are as diverse as individuals. The important thing is that you live in alignment with your life purpose.

You can explore the energies of your fixed design in meditation while reciting the Mantra and holding a focus on the energy of your fixed design for this lifetime. (You can substitute the phrase "perfect design" for fixed design if you are more comfortable with it). You will become clear on your life purpose, if that is your intention. Usually, once people discover their purpose and can realign their lives to serve their design, their lives begin to work better.

As you begin to recite the Mantra, there will be a few moments when very high level energies from your Soul flash down the antahkarana into your body and into your other energy system.

In those moments, there is a great deal of transformation occurring and much can be accomplished during that time. Furthermore, the effect is cumulative.

Remember, each time you do the Mantra you *permanently* raise the vibrational frequency of your energies. The physical body has to be transformed and transmuted before it can contain large amounts of your Soul's Light for long periods of time.

The energy of Soul can be used to accomplish many of your transformational goals. It will begin to clear and harmonize your emotional body, transform your cellular programming, raise the vibrations of your DNA and your atomic structure, and generally prepare you for the high level energies you will be experiencing.

As you repeat the Mantra it is important to begin to feel the energies of the different phrases. Becoming aware of subtle energies is extremely important and very growth enhancing. You and your body are a magnificent energy system far more complex than any other on this planet. The speed and ease with which you grow will depend to a large extent on you becoming aware of those subtle energies.

Reciting the Mantra while in a meditative state is the most effective way to use it, and you will generally experience the most intensity this way. However, you will benefit by using it under any circumstances. For example, it can also be used while walking or driving.

Learning to meditate is an important part of the transformational process and it is unlikely that you will be able to transform your energies and evolve to very high levels without first learning to meditate. Many people who have had difficulty meditating have used the Mantra to successfully deepen and improve their meditative abilities.

The simplest way to use the Mantra is to sit quietly with your eyes closed, perhaps listening to your favorite meditation music as you repeat the Mantra out loud or to yourself. In the beginning you may find it more effective to say it out loud. You may want to repeat the Mantra ten or fifteen times during a twenty to thirty minute meditation. You will quickly find what works best for you and make adjustments accordingly.

Always formulate your intention before you begin to meditate. As you journey in your meditations you can meet your guides, obtain answers to any questions you may have, and travel to other dimensions. This list is by no means complete. The more imaginative and creative you are at finding new ways to use the Soul Star, the faster you will grow and accomplish your goals.

The energy of your Soul Star will increase your awareness on a number of levels. Many people find that not long after they begin this process they become more aware of their guides and the multidimensional aspects of their Soul. Some even see and experience past lives, especially those lives with an emotional influence in this lifetime.

There is probably no other time when so much of your Soul's Light and energy is within your aura and in your body as when you are reciting the Soul Star Mantra. Your Soul is connected to the Universe and the universal mind, and learning to tap into that wisdom and information for use in your everyday life can be of great benefit to you. We know of many people who have experienced an increase in their inner knowing, psychic ability, clairvoyance, creativity and much more as a result of using the Soul Star Mantra in this way.

Another way to use the Mantra to enhance your experience is to hold in your awareness whatever it is that you wish to know more about. For instance, if you want the answer to a question, form the question and hold it in your awareness while repeating the Mantra. **As the Soul Star energies flash downward, with them comes the wisdom of your Soul, inner knowing, and the higher mind.**

The Soul Star can also be used to heal your body. If you have physical pain or want to heal an area of your body, hold a focus there while reciting the Mantra. Physical problems always have their origin in the psyche or emotional body. Holding the issue, pain, or physical problem in your awareness while repeating the Mantra will often create awareness of what the real problem is. If you are sick or have an injury, you can explore the reasons why you may have chosen that experience by using the Mantra. It is very important to the healing process to find out what hidden message is behind the injury or sickness. Sometimes this can go very deep, or even reach back into a former life. If you experience difficulty getting in touch with the root cause of a problem, you may find it useful to have a facilitator help you to bypass the defenses of your ego. It can be very helpful to have someone gently assist you as you begin to explore the regions of the subconscious and bring forth the light of awareness.

Awareness is always healing. When you become aware of the underlying emotional cause of the physical problem, healing will ensue. As you continue to do the Soul Star Mantra you are giving your Soul a tremendous opportunity to heal both your emotional body and your physical body. Soul knows how to heal you and how to transform your energies. If your intent is to heal and release old beliefs and stuck emotions, you can do so by using the Soul Star in your meditations. Your intent and desire to heal are powerful allies in the healing process. Energy always follows thought. Your thoughts and your intent will easily guide the energy of the Soul Star to those places where healing is necessary.

As you begin to explore those old beliefs, fears, and other issues that you want to release, you may be afraid that you will become overwhelmed and not know how to handle the issues that come up. Your Soul knows what is for your highest good and will never give you more than you can easily process at one time.

Your Soul is a Divine, loving, healing source of wisdom and energy, not a task master. If doing the Mantra brings up an issue and you feel you cannot deal with it, remember, it is just your ego's resistance. Ego is trying to trick you into believing that you can't handle it. Your Soul knows it is time to resolve the issue or It wouldn't have brought the issue to your awareness. Ego is clever at defending its turf. You have probably become adept in this lifetime and many others at avoiding your issues. During this time of transformation, it is becoming harder and harder to continue to do so. You might as well face your issues now while using the gentle, loving energy of your Soul to help transform and release them.

The energy of the Soul Star can appear very subtle compared with most of your third dimensional experiences of energy. It may be, however, that you are simply out of touch with higher frequencies such as the Soul Star, and as you become more aware of, and able to sense those energies, they will become more intense.

Working with others in a group is a good way to intensify your experience of the Soul Star. When you join with others to augment your experience you are also in alignment with the Divine plan for us to come together in unity and oneness. Those of us who have learned to use the Soul Star to effect change and to heal the emotional body are in no doubt that it is an immensely powerful technique. Even those who use the Mantra daily can still be inspired to awe and wonder that such a simple technique can be so effective.

When it comes to exploring your subconscious beliefs, fears and other issues, nothing is as powerful as the Soul Star Mantra. Major breakthroughs have been accomplished by many who have used the Soul Star process. One person became aware that he had an agreement at a subconscious level to perpetuate old familial patterns that were very abusive. The patterns were easily changed once they were brought to his awareness. Richard once worked with a woman who became aware of another lifetime where she had been persecuted for being psychic. This person desired a strong connection to her Soul, but every time she tried to increase her connection to Soul, she experienced intense fear. That pattern was also transformed while doing the Soul Star Mantra. Another woman was able to look at her issues around being sexually abused and was able to release them at the gentle urging of her Soul. Abuse issues are often hard to deal with without reliving much of the trauma. Using the loving energy of your Soul you can often transmute them with ease.

The following is an excerpt from Richard's book <u>Creating Your Light Body (p46)</u> which he co-authored with Richard Krull. In this excerpt the authors talk about how they discovered the power of the Soul Star to release old issues:

One Friday night the authors were sitting around talking about various issues including what new books or projects to start. It was our typical weekly get together in which we discussed metaphysical matters with great enthusiasm and intensity....

That night, our conversation led us to talk about a small group Dan (Richard Dan Dupuis) had recently joined. The participants in this group were working with various personal issues. Someone had asked Dan why he seemed to have to go over and over the anger around his mother's death many years ago. It had been an ongoing issue that seemed to be nearly impossible to resolve. The issue had come up in many ways in rebirthing sessions and workshops Dan had attended to look at issues. Yet it remained. Some of the charge had been eliminated but it still seemed to be a problem in his relationships from time to time.

That Friday evening when the authors were together, Dan asked Richard's Guide Aum-een about this issue and why the anger persisted after processing it time and time again. Aum-een suggested that Dan close his eyes and do a Soul Star Mantra that they had recently learned to enhance the connection to the Soul/High Self...

Shortly after igniting the Soul Star a couple of times by using the Soul Star Mantra, Richard's guide began to ask a series of questions related to how and why the anger served Dan. This went back and forth with questions and answers.

Aum-een asked Dan to do the Soul Star Mantra a couple of times during the dialogue. All of a sudden the answer was absolutely clear to Dan. It had been his subconscious choice to experience anger around his mother's death instead of experiencing or feeling the loss.

...The awareness that came out of the dialogue between Dan and Richard's guide, Aum-een, had suddenly created a shift that seemed to totally transmute the anger. The shift and movement around the energy of anger made us think that as an issue the anger was perhaps gone. This turned out to be true and a life long battle had been won in a few minutes and under what seemed to us as rather unusual circumstances.

A few days later working on some other issues and discussing them with someone else, Dan decided to try the Soul Star Mantra again as a way to obtain some insight. It worked again and significant insight into another long term issue was gained....

We began to experiment in various ways to find and release old issues by using the Soul Star Mantra to help bring them into awareness...

We believe anyone can use the Soul Star to gain insight. However, it seems to work better when there are two people; one with an issue to be resolved and one person as a facilitator. The one with the issues goes into a light meditative state and ignites the Soul Star by using the Soul Star Mantra. The facilitator asks questions about what the one with the issue is experiencing. The questions can be almost anything and the facilitator, using their intuitive ability and the Soul Star, will probably have a sense of the right questions to ask. Simple, open ended questions seem to be the most useful. Questions such as, " What are you experiencing?" "What are your thoughts?" "Do you understand the cause of the issue?"

It is important to note that anytime the dialogue slows, the one processing issues should do the Mantra again. The facilitator can indicate when to do the Mantra by repeating it slowly out loud.

If you are the facilitator do not be afraid of asking the wrong question. Remember that you also are using the power of your Soul/High Self. Soul is guiding the process whether or not you are aware of it. Even questions that do not seem to fit will cause the one doing the process to search for more information about the issue. If you are experimenting, you may wish to switch roles and have the facilitator work on issues while the other then becomes the facilitator. Don't be concerned if your first session seems ineffective. With practice you will see how useful and effective this process can be.

As we have developed this process, and discovered how powerful it really is at releasing issues, beliefs, fear and old outmoded psychological programs, we have discovered that it works because of several elements. When the Soul Star Mantra is used, the power and cooperation of the Souls of both the facilitator and the one working on an issue are being invoked. Soul provides the awareness. The awareness of the unconscious issue is the result of higher energies of Soul being infused into that part of the ego structure where the issue lies hidden. That brings it to the surface to be released.

This process seems to work especially well because of the connection at a soul level of the facilitator and the person working on the issue. This also provides the ability of the facilitator to intuit the right questions and understand what issues the one using the mantra is dealing with.

So far we have used the process with about every conceivable issue you can imagine. One of our clients discovered and released what appeared to be a contract, or agreement, with his father to carry forth his father's abusive behavior and beliefs...... The client had carried this contract for over fifty years and was able to release it in less than an hour.

People vary as to how they release and work on old issues. The important part to remember when doing this is that your Soul knows how to work with your energies and ego to transmute the issue. With some people, the release and transmutation of the energy occurs outside of their conscious awareness. This is not the norm but it does happen. With these people the shift is not noticed until the next day or so when they realize the issue is no longer part of their behavior and consciousness. Occasionally a core belief or issue takes two or three sessions to totally release. For those of us who have worked on issues time and time again, only to discover at some later date that we really didn't release the entire issue, this seems like a miracle....

It is well documented in the mainstream psychological community that the ego tends to rebuild its cherished defenses. One of the weaknesses of the system, and it is really not a weakness, is our tendency to think that if something is simple, it cannot succeed. Our culture seems to teach us that we have to struggle and work hard at everything to accomplish anything worthwhile. Because we think things have to take time and effort there is a tendency, even with the Soul Star Mantra system, for our ego to attempt to rebuild some of the old defenses and parts of the old programs. However the depth of the shift and the number of layers that have been peeled away from the issue is usually so great that anything that has been rebuilt can be easily dealt with in another session.

At first we could hardly believe the results we were getting. But over and over again, issues were released completely in one session and rarely did it take more than two or three.

Another interesting facet of what we are doing is that if we can create enough Soul charge and ask the right questions, a block of issues can be released without looking at each individual fragment of a gestalt of beliefs and issues......

Our Soul knows how to work with our ego and energy systems to do whatever is necessary to elicit a change without creating greater resistance. In fact, this may be the greatest strength of this process, its ability to bypass a lot of ego resistance. We have begun to experiment with raising the vibration of ego in order to transmute its lower frequencies. Our experience is that once the energy is transmuted and raised to a higher vibration, the negative charge is gone and the old thought patterns or belief systems are obliterated"....

Not only are you releasing fear and old blocks to growth, you are also raising the frequencies of your other energy systems at the same time. For us it is an answer to our requests and prayers to be part of the discovery of such a powerful, yet simple system that everyone can use. Of course, when you begin it may not flow freely at first, but with a little practice it will become an easy and invaluable tool.

Richard: " The Universe is bringing to us many new systems to work with that are short cuts. This is the simplest, yet one of the most powerful transformative techniques the authors have yet used in their search for faster, gentler and more efficient systems to release old issues, beliefs, programs, and fears.

Even more astounding is that each time you recite the Mantra, no matter what you are using it for, to gain awareness or to heal, you are raising your energy frequencies and permanently encoding more of your Soul's Light into your body and its energy field."

Chapter Four The Power of Invocation

A Message from Ashtar:

This is Ashtar, Shepherd for the Earth. At this time you are entering a crisis period on Earth. Because of the turbulence created by the ascension of your planet many of you are in personal crisis, know that this is a symptom of the larger crisis, the division between the Earth and its peoples.

As one who has the responsibility of shepherding the races through this time of travail I am concerned that not enough of you will align with the ascension of your planet to preserve mankind. Your Earth may become a fourth dimensional planet without a population to inhabit it. Far too few of you are aware at this time.

You have probably heard that there have been plans to evacuate the Earth as it begins to cleanse its surface and become inhospitable to its inhabitants. We would much rather see all of you do your own Ascension and become fourth dimensional along with the planet.

My friends, we are here to serve you in whatever capacity we can. You can call on us at any time. Many of you who are involved in your metaphysics, in your own process of awakening, were sent here from our ships, you are members of this Brotherhood of Light as it is often called. You have special assignments to perform, a mission if you will, to be of service to humanity and the Earth at this time. But as we have stated far too few of you have awakened to your part in this Divine plan, too many of you who are designated Light Workers and Starseeds who have come here to serve have not heard the call and are still asleep.

Of course many of you are beginning to feel the stirring, your Divine coding is calling you to awaken at this time. Those stirrings are your time clock, your wake up call. Those of you scheduled to awaken at this time will have to work very hard not to awaken and heed this call.

Why would you be so deeply asleep? Because you have become addicted to the emotional energies of this planet. Your emotional body is synchronized to the emotional rhythms of the Earth. Your ego structure has come to believe that this three dimensional planet is its home. Your ego's are intractable.

At a Soul level you have invoked these changes, you have invoked the aid of the Universe and the brotherhood to assist you. Now it is time for you to awaken to your Soul's invocation and to consciously, en masse join in this invocation.

The power of Invocation is an invaluable tool of awakening because it is in alignment with your own Soul's inherent capacity to make use of it. It is a tool given to you and your Soul by the Brotherhood that will not and cannot fail you when used with sincerity and integrity. Use it with our blessing.

Throughout history many powerful methods of healing have come and gone, along with the cultures and civilizations that have used them. Often great works and teachings like the Dead Sea Scrolls have been virtually lost along with their wisdom and mysterious powers. Today intellectual and logical thought is valued above all else. Many of the old teachings have been neglected as though wisdom and knowledge were *our* birthright and ours alone.

We assume that we are somehow more advanced because we have access to modern technologies. Through man's arrogance, many potentially powerful and effective healing systems have been relegated to the dingy recesses of history and posterity.

The process of invocation reaches into antiquity, and is as ancient as the development of language itself. Like so many other ideas and concepts it was almost lost to us because it didn't seem to fit with contemporary thoughts and ideas. An anachronism, it appeared to be part of an ancient mystic tradition of magicians and sorcerers that was no longer appropriate.

Many ancient traditions, however, are now being 'rediscovered' as powerful tools for transformation. There are few techniques, if any, as simple and yet as effective as invocation. One of the main reasons is this: energy follows thought and the spoken word is even more powerful in the way that it determines your reality. As you begin to use invocation you will be amazed at just how effective it can be. Through invocation alone you can heal your life and radically alter your experience and perception of reality.

Richard: "The following provides a vivid example of just how powerful invocation can be. I had been working with the Soul Star Mantra, exploring its potential and its power while also working with my Light Body. Your Light Body is your Soul's radiation and ordinarily it is not able to come into this dimension because of the density of the energies. I had heard that certain electromagnetic energies help make the Light Body self igniting.

The inference was that my Light Body could be constantly activated. It seemed like a logical next step for me. Instead of always having to ignite my Light Body during meditation, it would simply always be on and doing its transformative work. It takes quite a bit of practice and meditation to get anywhere near this point of activation. By the time I recognized self activation as a real possibility, I was already very experienced at handling the energies of the Light Body and my other energy systems.

One night while sitting in meditation, I thought I would try this grand experiment. I decided to see whether I could speed up the process of self activation by using invocation and simultaneously working with the energies of my Light Body.

I sat in meditation for ten minutes or so, playing with the Light Body frequencies. I did the Soul Star Mantra a number of times until I felt connected to the Light Body and the Soul Star. Then I invoked the specific frequencies that would help make my Light Body self igniting. The particular frequencies I was invoking are similar to electricity. (We are not completely identifying these frequencies because to prematurely invoke them can be hazardous to your health and physical well being, and maybe even your survival.) I repeated the invocation a number of times. Wow! This was getting more and more intense, just the way I like it. Suddenly there was a tremendous surge of energy. It was so powerful that I became uncomfortable. I stopped invoking the energy and came out of my meditation.

I didn't understand at that point why I had become so uncomfortable. Nor was I very concerned over what had happened. A little while later I went to bed. When I woke up the next morning I had a tremendous fever, I felt as though I was burning up. The fever lasted for three days. I suspected that the fever was a result of the energy I had been invoking the previous day. My guides confirmed that this was true.

That fever turned out to be the direct result of overloading my physical circuits with the particular frequencies of energy I had been working with. My guides also warned me that I could indeed overload my body with those energies to the point where the physical body would not survive. *Under ordinary circumstances there is never any risk that you will come to any harm using these invocations."*

Your ability to bring in and integrate higher frequencies of Light and energy sets the pace for your evolution. The process of transformation and evolution includes working with your personal energies, such as those of your aura, your emotional and mental bodies and with the energy of your cell's DNA and the atoms that make up your physical body.

Ordinarily your ability to work with your cell's DNA and atomic structure are somewhat restricted, however, using these techniques you can reach deep inside your DNA and atomic structures and raise the frequencies which emanate from the very atoms that make up who you are.

For those who decide to work with and become aware of their higher energies the rewards are tremendous. As you enhance your connectedness to these energies, the wisdom and knowledge you can access will greatly expand. Everyone who is willing to work with their energies will experience greater awareness of all kinds and an increased ability to heal themselves and others.

The most important step in all of this is to increase your connection to Soul's Light and energy.

The more you are able to bring in Soul's energies, the more you will experience healing and Soul's qualities in your life. It is important to note that all positive qualities and characteristics, the ones we most admire in ourselves and others, are Soul characteristics. You may have thought that they were aspects of personality or ego, but they are not. The personality may adopt them, but it obtains them from Soul.

Love is perhaps the most profound of Soul qualities. The energy of love radiates forth from your Soul and is the basis of all healing. Some of the other characteristics of Soul are harmony, abundance, wisdom, honesty, integrity and courage. Soul does not know fear or indeed any other negative trait.

The invocation we recommend to increase your connection to your Soul's Light and energy is incredibly simple, as indeed are all of our invocations. You may find many complex invocations in other books. However, they are usually very cumbersome to use, particularly if you are trying to memorize them or read them while holding a meditative state.

This is one of our favorite invocations:

IN THE NAME AND WISDOM OF SOUL
I INVOKE A STRONGER CONNECTION
TO MY SOUL'S LIGHT AND ENERGY.

We always begin the invocation with the phrase 'In the name and wisdom of Soul I invoke.................' This key phrase is the work horse of the system. *Make no mistake, in spite of its simplicity, there is no more powerful combination of words on this dimension.*

In order to work effectively with invocation, sit quietly in a meditative state for a few minutes, reciting to yourself or out loud the Soul Star Mantra. As you begin to feel more and more relaxed and connected to your Soul Star, recite the Mantra. Do this several times. Could anything be simpler? Continued practice will enable you to greatly enhance your connection to Soul's Light and your Soul. As you continue to work with this process you will begin to feel a profound transformation of your energies at deep inner levels.

It is possible to invoke almost any energy and experience that you care to imagine. For instance, later in this book we refer to the process of Ascension. You can actually invoke the energy of Ascension as well as that of your Light Body, or even the energy of your guides. Or anything else you can think of for that matter. If you can conceptualize it and speak of it you can invoke it. Be creative, try other things that you sense intuitively will work for you.

Invocation is really very simple, in fact you may be wondering what is so remarkable about it. When used in the way we recommend, invocation provides a laser-like intensity of focus to whatever your intent is and to those things that you are working on.

Invocation opens a pathway for the Light of your Soul to enter into the deepest recesses of your entire energy system. According to a law of physics, the Law of Entropy, higher frequencies always transmute lower frequencies. The Light of Soul will transmute your energies. There is no exception to this Law.

You can use the power of the Mantra and invocation to change your reality, and thereby improve any area of your life that is not working. You might wish to improve your finances, your relationships or even your health.

When you wish to make changes to the physical body, invoke the energy that you are working with into your DNA and atomic structure. For example:

IN THE NAME AND WISDOM OF SOUL I INVOKE.... THE ENERGY OF ASCENSION...... INTO MY DNA AND THE ATOMS OF MY PHYSICAL BODY.

You can insert almost any word you can think of where we have used the word "Ascension".

Invocation is the simplest and most powerful technique we have ever come across. Used independently or in combination with other transformational tools and techniques - particularly the Soul Star Mantra, it will greatly speed and enhance your evolutionary process.

Chapter Five The Emotional Body

A Message from Ra Ta:

You are probably all aware that you have an emotional body. Of course you are aware of that because you can feel the turbulence in your emotions as you read this information.

That is how you know you have an emotional body because you can feel your emotions. Without your emotional body you would not resemble a member of the human race. Other races do not have emotional bodies, most in fact do not. You can view that as privilege or curse. Your emotional bodies make you uniquely human.

On Earth you have your wonderful emotional body which allows you to perceive your reality in an entirely different way than on any other planet or in any other Universe.

Of course, because of this increased sensitivity to your surroundings, it is also important that you keep your emotional body very clear and harmonized. Your emotional body is a tool that enables you to have awareness and perception, but it is also very sensitive to thought. Your thoughts very quickly disrupt its energy and flow, and therefore you must not have a lot of discordant thoughts or your emotional body will be out of harmony. Harmony, as you are about to find out if you do not know already, is very important to your emotional body.

If your emotional body has become a receptacle for your discordant thoughts throughout this lifetime you are going to have to clean It out in order to have the growth you desire.

As your evolution progresses you will actually transcend the need to have an emotional body, and the lower three chakras and the emotional body will indeed become obsolete in a fourth dimensional environment. This is not to say that your emotional bodies have not been a grand experiment and a wonderful tool for experiencing a wide range of feelings, but as you raise your consciousness you will simply turn elsewhere for the perception you have gained through your emotional body.

The emotional body is an energy body which extends six to eight feet beyond your physical body and is cylindrical in shape. Beyond that is your mental body. They rotate around one another and have a specific harmonic, or ratio of spin, relative to each other. Although they are earth energy systems, they do not have mass and are not made up of atoms like the physical body.

These very fine subtle energies are etheric in nature, and are quite easily influenced by your environment and your thoughts. The alignment of the energies of your emotional and mental bodies is important to your growth and daily existence. If you are to continue your Spiritual growth it is imperative that you work with and understand the energies of the emotional body.

If you did not have an emotional body, you would be like a computer or automaton, unable to sense, feel, or emote; some of the most basic elements of your human experience would simply be missing. You would lack that most fundamental experience, the ability to feel love. The way that we as humans feel, emote and experience love is highly distinctive. It is our emotions and feelings that distinguish us from the animal kingdom.

Much of your personality is defined by your emotional body. The way an individual displays emotions or deals with other people's emotions is highly characteristic of that individual. Your emotional body helps identify you as the unique individual that you are.

If you are to respond to, rather than be controlled by, your emotions, then the energies of the emotional body must be organized and able to flow freely. For most people, those energies are not flowing freely. That is because of a very human tendency to suppress your emotions so that you do not have to deal with them.

Virtually everyone suppresses their emotions to some extent. There may be times when you are suppressing your emotions and are not aware of it because on the surface you appear to be stable and relatively calm. It is important that you begin to recognize when you are doing that. By continuing to suppress those energies, you will build up a charge that will have to be released sooner or later. When that charge erupts you will most likely appear (and be) very unstable! The only times when you are truly emotionally stable are those when the flow of energies is constant, harmonious and balanced throughout your emotional and mental bodies.

Because of their close association, anything that affects the emotional body also affects the mental body. When the emotional body energies are in harmony, the mental body can function with ease. The ratio of spin which exists between the two bodies must be constant so that energy and information can readily be transferred from one to the other.

As we have said the energies can easily become distorted, particularly when you try to suppress emotions and feelings. When that happens the ratio between the two alters and interferes with communication. Also, suppression can and usually does, distort the shape of the emotional body adding to the problem.

Although the link between the two bodies is not well understood, it is easily demonstrated. You will no doubt have observed how anxiety and other emotional disturbances can affect your mental processes. You cannot think as clearly as when you are calm and centered.

The way that we respond when our emotional body is out of harmony is somewhat instinctive. There is a natural tendency for the emotional body to want to vent in order to reorganize itself. The energies of the emotional body are to a certain extent, self regulating, in that it always attempts to be in harmony.

By suppressing the energies of your emotional body you can convince yourself, albeit temporarily, that you are in a state of harmony. However, before long, when it is disorganized and lacking in harmony, the emotional body will reorganize itself by *venting*. When it does so, it may not be very discriminating as to when it vents and on whom! For that reason if no other, it is a good idea not to let the energy charge get to the point where it vents indiscriminately.

Venting emotion can, of course, be a very good way to reorganize the emotional body. Feelings and emotions need to be expressed, released and vented, not stored or suppressed. However this needs to be done in a way that is safe for you and those around you. Venting your feelings on others is not a good way to liberate emotions. Working with others in groups can be an excellent way to do emotional release work.

We also recommend rebirthing as a highly effective tool for restoring feelings and emotions. It as an excellent yet simple process which works with the breath. As a child you may well have learned to suppress your natural spontaneity through your breath. Being spontaneous in most families is unacceptable. When Richard began his own healing, rebirthing was one of the first healing processes he was drawn to, and he now uses this technique to help others reclaim their own emotions and feelings.

Bringing harmony to the emotional body can be accomplished in a number of ways. Those of you who understand chakras and have worked with them may find it beneficial to work with the lower three centers, especially the second chakra. Those centers are connected to the emotional body. Try invoking the Light of your higher self/Soul into your second chakra and the emotional body; this will begin to transmute the lower energies. Harmonizing the lower chakras will enable you to harmonize the energies of the emotional body, and as you begin to move higher energies into the emotional body they will push lower energies up and out.

When that happens it will probably trigger your own emotions and feelings. Let those emotions run. You are simply making way for higher energies. When you begin to feel calm and centered again, continue working with whatever technique helps you to restore balance in the emotional body.

It has been said that there are really only two emotions, love and fear. There may or may not be other true emotions, but you will almost certainly be aware of the different polarities of those two emotions and how they can affect you. You are only able to truly feel and express love when you have harmony in your emotional body.

The emotional body is the receptacle for the experience of love on this dimension. It experiences the energy of love as a feeling. The emotional body also contains the energy of fear, and when fear is the predominant emotion you cannot express or experience love.

Fear will block the feeling and expression of love. It will cause your emotional body to shut down, making it inaccessible to love and indeed any other positive emotions and feelings. Fear cannot coexist simultaneously with love.

The emotion which predominates on this plane is fear. We often see the flip side of fear, which is anger, being expressed, but that is just a different way of expressing the same thing. You will doubtless be able to think of many other emotional states, but none are as prevalent as fear or its counterpart, anger. Most people have a predisposition towards one or the other. There may be some who are centered and balanced, but the majority are not.

For much of our recorded history, the various cultures and

civilizations of the world have been essentially fear based. Almost everyone finds it difficult to maintain harmony in the emotional body, and thus remain connected to the higher energies that contain the frequency of love. There is so much fear in the energies that surround us that frequently the emotional body is responding to someone else's fear. It is not even yours! It is essential that you continuously add the energies of harmony to your emotional body in order to combat all the fear and anger that you unknowingly receive from other sources.

Fear had its origin as a physiological response to danger, it kept us safe by enabling us to run away from predators and other enemies. That time has long since passed; however, the legacy lives on.

Ego has claimed fear as its own. Increasingly, ego's way of viewing the world we live in is fear based.   In other words, ego uses fear to filter our reality. Many of us have even learned to fear love. This is in large measure the result of living in dysfunctional families and being shut down by our parents when we tried to express our love for them.

Parents tend to accept love conditionally, on their terms. If we do not meet their expectations they will not accept our expressions of love. The resultant distortion has had a tremendous impact on the way in which we perceive our reality. Needless to say, it is an unnecessary and weighty burden for our emotional bodies.

An emotional body which is overwhelmed with the energy of fear vibrates at lower and lower frequencies and finds itself even further removed from the higher frequencies of love.

It is becoming more and more important to maintain harmony in the emotional body so that we can incorporate and integrate the higher energies of transformation that we are receiving at this time. When you are consistent in organizing and harmonizing those energies, they are transmuted to higher frequencies.

Your emotional body defines so much of your reality that perhaps no other energy system is as fundamental to your growth and existence. If you simply released fear entirely from the emotional body, the incoming energy of love would be all that was necessary to completely transform your energies to very high frequencies. You would experience only bliss and love.

Our thoughts, emotions and feelings are the basic currency from which we create our reality. Emotions propel thoughts into reality; the more intense the emotion or feeling the quicker it manifests. If the fundamental or predominant energies of your emotional body are fear, then you will manifest more experiences of that nature.

Consequently, if there is a lot of fear in your emotional body, **you will manifest that which you fear most,** instead of what you really want.

Clearing and harmonizing the emotional body is an important growth step whether you are preparing for Ascension or pursuing Spiritual growth of any kind. Or even if you simply want to make your life work better.

We have stressed over and over that one of the most important skills you can develop is the ability to work with and sense energy. It does not matter how you do that, whether you actually sense energy or just know what the energy is doing. If you are unable at this time in your growth and development to sense or feel your energies, you can use your imagination or just pretend. Either way is equally effective.

For example, suppose that you are feeling anxiety or some other disturbance in the energies of your emotional body. Close your eyes, go into meditation and try to become aware of the blocked energy. Sometimes you may not be able to do so. If you cannot, make a symbol or pretend that you have found the blocked or distorted energies. That is all you need do.

Your energies have an intelligence all of their own, they will follow your intent and desire. After finding the energy or making a symbol for it, do the Soul Star Mantra, while holding the distorted or blocked energy in your awareness.

The higher energies of your Soul Star will transmute those

lower energies. The Law of Entropy states that higher energies always transmute lower energies. When you are working with extremes of energy, very low and very high energies, you will have to repeat the process several times, because to some extent the higher energies will be lowered as they raise the lower energies.

The emotional body also plays a critical role in the etiology of physical disease. So called *physical* disease isn't really physical at all, it has its origin in emotional disturbance.

Disease is **always** the result of distorted energies. Energies that are blocked or stifled, like stagnant water are not conducive to health and vitality. Disease and other ailments are the result of subconscious disturbances that affect your energies. If you concentrate on finding the underlying belief or thought behind the problem, you will find that this is always the case.

A man whose tear ducts were not working came to Richard for healing. The telepathic message Richard received from that man's subconscious was "I will never cry again." An early experience which had been very traumatic had brought about that response and it had remained with him for decades. This example is typical of how our thoughts and emotions affect the physical body.

When you are experiencing physical problems, you can usually uncover the subconscious thought that created the imbalance in your energies. You can use the various techniques we describe in order to do this.

One very effective way is to hold your awareness on the area of your body where the problem exists and do the Soul Star Mantra. It may take several attempts, but you will get your answer. The awareness that this creates may in itself be enough to start the healing process.

While reading this chapter on the emotional body, you may find yourself in resistance to the information, or feeling angry. For many, reading or thinking about these issues begins to bring them to the surface.

There is no better time to begin looking at your emotional

body to see what is up for you, and to begin transmuting these energies.

Richard: "While writing the chapter on Fear of Growth in my other book Creating Your Light Body, my co-author became so embroiled in his own fear and issues that he had to set it aside. It was not until we had almost finished the book, that he was able to complete that chapter. You may experience a similar dilemma while reading this chapter and the next one. We recommend that you do not allow your fear or your anger to control you.

It is time for you and all Light Workers to stand fast and conquer your fear. If you don't, you simply will not be part of the transformation of yourself and the planet."

Ego can be very intractable because it is the guardian of your beliefs and the status quo. Ego will see your fear, anger, beliefs and other issues as part of your reality and therefore will be resistant to changing them; that is, after all, its job, as the guardian of your reality. However, ego can be retrained, old patterns and beliefs changed, and fear transmuted. Fear, after all, is just energy and as you already know, those lower energies can be transmuted by the higher energy of your Soul Star.

Working with the emotional body, your emotions and your feelings, is fundamental to healing. You cannot ignore this step and expect to heal your life. If you believe that you are to be part of this transformation and the ascension of this planet, then you must work with your emotional body in preparation.

The emotional body is the foundation from which all healing begins. You may begin somewhere else, but no matter where you start, you will be brought back to face the issues that affect your emotional body.

Chapter Six Feelings

A Message from Ra-Sha, Spokesman for the Pleiadian Hierarchy

Our relationship with your planet has been close and intimate for the eons of your existence, we have watched over the development of your various cultures and civilizations since the beginning of time on your planet.

We are intimately familiar with the workings of your energy bodies in a way that is only possible because of the manner in which we hold the basic planes of your existence .

There are seven planes for all levels or dimensions. It is our job to see to it that the planes are constant in their vibration. We do this without effort or thought, we do it through what you would call intent.

At the present time your ability to access the planes lies in the nature of your feelings.   Because your Soul is multidimensional it is important for you to be able to access those multi dimensions.

In the past this was not nearly as important as it is now, because you are at a stage of accelerated growth and beginning to bridge the dimensions of your consciousness. Your feelings very much form this connection to those other dimensions of Soul. You tend to ignore your feeling nature for your mental nature. You will indeed transcend your emotional feeling nature but for now it is vastly important to reawaken your feelings. It will not always be fun but it will be very rewarding and beneficial to do so. We speak to you out of concern and compassion for your individually and as a race. We have been asked by your planetary Hierarchy to assist in any way we can to inform and educate you to your own nature. Why? Because you are Pleiadian. Not all of you of course are originally from the Pleiades but the vast majority of you are. You will feel and know if this is so for you as you read this.

We of course are not special . There are many others who have come from different star systems, but because of the great numbers of Pleiadians on this planet we have been asked to step up our broadcast to you.

We say unto you that there is only one thing you must do to awaken your dormant feelings and energies. Allow. Give up your desire for control of your feelings and you will experience and grow beyond your ability to imagine it.

Like a radio station that uses different bands and frequencies to transmit and receive information, you are also an electromagnetic sender and receiver. This is only an analogy, of course; you are far more complex and powerful than any radio yet conceived.

Your electromagnetic energies are capable of transcending time and space and receiving information from other dimensions. You have the innate ability to access those dimensions, bring forth information from them and interpret it through your feelings and their connection to your Soul. The potential you have to do this is far in excess of anything that you currently utilize or may even be consciously aware of. Yet perhaps you have a sense of this untapped potential deep within.   Unlocking your feelings will restore your long forgotten capacity to transcend space and time and to access this reality with awe inspiring accuracy.

It is your body and the feelings that you have that are your Soul's antenna. In order for your Soul to be able to function as an effective antenna, your feelings must be able to flow freely throughout your body and your energies. Like any antenna it must be unobstructed in order to function properly. Any disturbance in your body and its energies can, and will, limit its ability to receive and transmit the information that you receive via your feelings.

There are other information systems that are used by Soul also, but none are anywhere near as important as your feelings. With this system freely receiving and transmitting, guidance will always be readily forthcoming. Like a cat without whiskers, you are groping in the dark when your feelings are not flowing. You cannot interpret your reality. In effect, your primary guidance system is unavailable.

Little is known about how feelings and emotions operate. Of course the system is complex, but that in itself is not the reason why you know so little about your feelings. If you were able to retrace your own personal history you would probably discover that first your family and then other cultural influences discouraged the expression of your feelings. You took this to mean that you could not trust your feelings, and that the feelings were somehow inappropriate.

Many people are afraid of their feelings. For some of you, allowing yourself to actually feel your feelings may seem impossible. Why? Because as a child you thought that if you expressed your feelings you would meet such strong opposition that you would be abandoned, hurt or even killed by those who opposed your feelings.

If underlying your resistance to feeling and emotion you

hold the subconscious belief that to feel is to be hurt or even to die, it is no wonder that you have trouble expressing those feelings.

Intentionally or unintentionally, you began to mistrust your feelings. The net effect of this was that you began to lose touch with your feelings in early childhood. Whether or not this was a conscious choice really does not matter, what matters is that you are going to have to decide whether or not you are going to reestablish that trust. Reestablishing trust in your feelings is of primary importance to growth. Feelings never lie, they can only be misinterpreted. Your body knows what is true for you, but it is up to you to trust the information and act accordingly.

The following is a quote from Barbara Marciniak's excellent book <u>Bringers of the Dawn</u>, (page 153):

> Understand that your feelings are your ticket to ride into multidimensional realities, where you must go if you are seriously playing this game. In multidimensional realities, you learn to hold and focus many versions of yourself at once.
>
> Feelings can take you to these places, particularly the feelings that you trust. Many of you are very suspicious and masterful over your feelings. You will not allow certain feelings to come forward, or you judge them when they come up instead of observing where they take you or what they do for you.

Feelings are expressed through emotion. Emotions give voice to your feelings. Feelings are energy in motion, *e-motion*. It is emotion that enables you to keep that energy, the energy you have invested in your feelings, moving and flowing. The fuel that enables you to move your feelings and the emotional body is emotion. Without the addition of that fuel you cannot move and change direction. Without ignition, emotions remain static and unmoving, and you are unable to grow. It is as simple as that.

When your emotions and feelings are stuck, you are stuck. Everyone experiences being blocked emotionally from time to time, especially those on an accelerated growth path like the one you are most probably on now. In order to get going again you will probably have to find a way to release yet another layer of feelings and emotions.

As we have said, almost without exception you are taught that your feelings and emotions are inappropriate in some way. Boys are taught not to cry and girls are taught that expressing anger is wrong. It is not surprising that the expression of feelings becomes almost impossible.

Men in this culture often do not know what feelings are, or whether in fact they even have feelings. Furthermore, we live in a male dominated society which values masculine qualities above feminine at the expense of our feeling nature. Prior to patriarchy, which dates back about three thousand years, most cultures were matriarchal and female qualities were valued over male qualities. That was not a viable option either.

Balance is preferred and that seems to be what we are moving towards as this evolutionary cycle comes to a close. Much progress has been made to correct the imbalance and yet, the fact remains that most men and women are unwilling and/ or unable to express their deepest fears and emotions.

This imbalance has affected our energies, especially those of the chakras. In general, the throat chakra for women and the heart chakra for men. The throat chakra is the vehicle for the expression of feelings, the heart chakra is the receptor for the feeling of love. It is important to recreate a flow in those energies if you are to re-establish your feeling nature.

In order to sense and feel love the heart chakra has to be

open. A closed heart chakra is common in men, but women also shut down their heart chakras, usually as a result of emotional pain and trauma. Indeed, it is unusual to find anyone who has not somewhat closed their heart chakra.

Love is a feeling. At least, that is the way it is interpreted by the emotional body. Many people do not experience love. Why? Because if you have shut down your feeling nature, or are suppressing your emotions and feelings, you have closed the door that allows the experience to manifest. It is an incredible tragedy for mankind that for most the experience of love is fleeting.

Love is an essential human need, a basic requirement like food or water. If you are not experiencing love, you will seek to fill the void in other ways. You will probably turn to symbolic substitutes. Sex, alcohol, drugs and over eating are often addictive substitutes for real love. The satisfaction that you experience from those addictions will only be temporary and cannot replace your innate need to experience the feeling of love.

Decades after Freud and others have explained how we try to fill our unfilled childhood needs symbolically, it is still believed by many people that we can correct our addictions and other habitual behaviors without involving our feelings. It simply will not happen unless you restore the body's ability to feel. When you begin to feel, you begin to feel and experience the love that your Soul and the Universe has for you.

Love is a quality of Soul. When we experience love in this dimension, it is from one Soul to another Soul. That connection cannot occur without the free and uninterrupted flow of feelings. In order to heal your life you are going to have to restore your ability to feel and emote. There is no alternative.

Once you retreat from the opportunity to express your feelings you make it harder to express them in the future. As an adult you understand intellectually there is really nothing to fear, no one will abandon you or harm you. You either face that fear by standing your ground and expressing your feelings, or you retreat into the darkness of your fears.

There are many ways to vent your emotions and feel your feelings that are perfectly harmless. If you are very reluctant to feel fear and vent your emotions, you probably need the support of a group. Groups are always co-created. When you enter a group, it will be with people just like you. They will show you tremendous empathy and support because they will recognize in you their own experience. Group support will allow you to go much deeper into your emotions than you can go without support.

This is another excerpt from <u>Bringers of the Dawn</u> (page 152) that speaks of this dilemma:

> It's not that you don't know how to feel, it's that you are afraid of your feelings. You don't know what to do with them when you have them. They bring up a sense of powerlessness within you, so you associate feeling with a sense of, " Oh, no, I blew it."
>
> You have a boundary in your belief system that states that when something comes up that is emotional and brings pain or anger, then it is not good. It is time to stop tiptoeing around things and avoiding your emotions.

Your ego is an emanation of your body. Your ego's role is to protect your body from external threats. As we have evolved, we have given it domain over our feelings. It determines which feelings are "OK" and which are not. Those "OK" feelings are the ones your family and parents would permit in early childhood. In most families feelings of all kinds are not permitted.

It takes work to restore those feelings, but when you do you will find that it is worth the effort. Not only will you begin to see the world around you in a different way, but your relationships will change to reflect the positive changes that you have made.

Richard: "My introduction to my own feelings came as a result of some rather unusual circumstances. Some years ago I met a woman who was doing rebirthing, an emotional release technique that at the time I had not heard of. It seemed interesting but that was as far as it went. A few weeks later I was at a seminar learning how to channel my higher self and do channeled writing.

While channeling for someone else my higher self took the opportunity to speak to me. A voice said in no uncertain terms 'Richard needs to do rebirthing'. My inner voice had chosen to speak to me about this while in a highly energized group setting where it would be hard for me to ignore the message.

Some weeks later I experienced rebirthing for myself. Rebirthing definitely tends to bring up your emotions and feelings After only a couple of sessions I had what I call a *primal scream*, and it is probably no coincidence that shortly before I had read Dr. Arthur Janov's excellent book The Primal Scream.

The process he calls Primal Therapy seems to me to be very similar to rebirthing. Rebirthing was an incredibly healing experience for me. You can become so adept at expressing your feelings and emotions that it becomes a non event, no more out of the ordinary or inconvenient than sneezing. I recommend it to anyone who sincerely wants to get in touch with their feelings."

It is really no mystery why people find it difficult to heal and to change. Ego regards any attempts to change the status quo as highly threatening. This incredible intractability of ego is the reason it is so hard to explore your feelings, doing so always creates change and is confrontive to ego.

Ego is very clever at preventing you from experiencing your feelings. Ego's main defense is fear. Ego will bring up a wall of fear every time you approach your feelings and try to change.

Fear itself cannot hurt you, it is simply an energy with a particular set of frequencies, designed to cause the body to flee. If you are not experiencing a physical threat, however, there is no need to withdraw. We are conditioned to withdraw physically or emotionally when our fears arise, and you have probably become quite proficient at doing so.

Every time you avoid your fear you increase the illusion that it is real. So, you have to learn a new response - to hold your ground and face your fear. You will be surprised at just how easy it is once you become accustomed to standing your ground when your fears arise.

Facing your fear can initially create a great deal of emotional upheaval. But remember that it is just what you need to do.

That is, if you truly desire to heal your life. If not, forget about all this healing stuff, stop reading at this point and carry on the way you have been. The choice is yours.

Everyone has certain issues around which there is a lot of fear and resistance. It takes a special effort to release that fear.

Fear and resistance are essentially the same thing. Ego uses fear to prevent you from experiencing the underlying feeling and any attendant emotion it perceives as negative.

One good way to deal with your fears is through your intellect, by learning to think differently about them. By using logical thought you can effectively deplete the energy of fear. When your fears are illogical, as they often are, speak to them, tell them they are being silly, that they are not making any sense, and there is really nothing to fear.

When you find an area where your fears are particularly resistant to mental effort you can use the Soul Star Mantra to soften and release them. You will find the Soul Star Mantra very effective for transmuting your fears.

More often than not, fear is really one of ego's smoke screens.

It is an attempt to cause you to change directions, to avoid the underlying issue. This trick of ego is very effective.

Our culture is adept at avoidance techniques. This is often the reason for many addictions and other neurotic behaviors. Many psychologists point out that it is not fear that is the problem. It is our avoidance of fear and feeling that creates the problem and produces such strange and often bizarre behaviors. One of the most common of these is incessant talking. Those who react this way are afraid that if they stop talking they will have to face their fear and other issues. The constant drone of their own voice numbs them to their feelings.

Another learned behavior the culture sanctions is that many people become incredibly analytical and logical the minute someone confronts their fears. This is very common, the entire culture seeming to flee into their heads as soon as someone or something brings up their fear or other issues.

Perception is also involved in how we process emotions. There is a common perception that it is painful to express feelings and emotions, that those old memories will hurt. Whether they are old emotions, hurts or memories, the perception is that bringing them to the surface and releasing them will hurt. This is an illusion created by ego, the pain is in the resistance, not in catharsis or release.

We repeat, the pain is in the resistance, not in the release.

Think about how it feels when you resist your body's natural tendency towards catharsis and release. Catharsis and release are the way your body cleanses itself. Those old stuffed feelings are contaminating your body and your energies. They need to be released.

Your body always responds positively to catharsis. It is just your perception that bringing those old feelings to the surface and releasing them will hurt. You will always have a sense of relief when you release old suppressed feelings and emotions.

Probably everyone has suppressed some feelings. There are times when emotion and feelings just do not seem appropriate, or so we tell ourselves. This may seem harmless enough at the time. However, those and all other suppressed feelings will always surface sooner or later as you heal and clear your emotional body.

Richard: "I had a most unusual experience while bicycling one day. I cycled past my old high school as I had done many times before, however this time I took a different route and went right by the entrance. As I went past the entrance I suddenly began to feel a lot of old hurt and feelings that I did not know were there.

My high school days seemed like a big lark to me consciously, but as that old hurt came up I realized there were many times I had suppressed a lot of painful feelings. I stopped bicycling and let the hurt surface. There were a lot of tears mixed with those old suppressed feelings."

Dealing with your emotions and feelings may be something you want to put off to a later date, maybe even until another lifetime. There is certainly no rule that says you have to explore and work with your feelings in this lifetime. You can try to put it off as long as you want to. However, it is an essential part of growth to release old stuck energies, feelings and emotions.

Sooner or later, in this lifetime or the next, you will have to take this walk; so you might just as well do it now.

The all knowing Universe is well aware of our tendency to avoid what seems unpleasant. So it has provided us with reflections, or mirrors. The people in our lives reflect back to us those areas we need to heal. They are our partners, our children, our colleagues and others who push our buttons and cause us to lose control of our feelings and emotions.

The primary reason for relationships is that of reflection. This is a very important part of your reality and something you should pay close attention to. It is a short cut to healing. When you are working on those issues presented to you in your relationships you are taking the shortest possible route to healing.

It is really a great gift to have those reflections and button pushers in your life. It may not seem that way in the heat of battle and conflict, but it is a gift from the Universe that you can use to guide you in your healing process. It can be very useful to reflect on the issues that come up during personal conflicts with others and to use it to your advantage.

As you begin to explore your feelings and release those old pent up emotions, your perception of the world around you will reflect the inner changes that you have made, and you will find that your life begins to work much better.

A Message from Bartholomew:

How do you create your beliefs my friends? You do not actually create them, you borrow them just as you would borrow sugar from your neighbor, perhaps a little more subtly than that, but you do get your beliefs from someone else: usually your parents, your family, your schools and other outside authorities you see as your teachers.

It is a natural thing to do, how else could you form your beliefs about a reality you are born into and know nothing about? Of course you would obtain your beliefs from those entrusted to teach you truth about the nature of your reality. So where did they get their beliefs from, the ones they so earnestly thrust upon you? From the same sources, parents family, schools etc.

Your beliefs may shift and change from childhood but your core beliefs about the nature of reality shift very little, if at all. Those core beliefs are strongly defended by the majority of the people you come in contact with.

Did your parents stop to examine the beliefs they passed on to you? Probably not; it is entirely likely that no one in your lineage has stopped to check them for truth for generations.

It is just too much work along with all the other

tasks at hand one must do just to survive.

What about you? Have you stopped to examine your beliefs? Or do you just carry them around with you like so much old baggage? They are just that you know, old baggage, decades, generations of old baggage, that create for you the reality you experience day after day, year after year.

Take an inventory of what you do believe. Are you even conscious of what your beliefs are? Probably not. You absorb them rather unconsciously and you pass them on without giving them the once over.

Those of you who are the vanguard of this evolution are beginning to wonder just what it is that creates such a chaotic planet. Your inner knowing is beginning to sense a greater truth, really an old truth, one that has been held in abeyance until such time as you desired to discover it.

Where can you find that new /old truth? Buried beneath the layers of that baggage that you carry around with you that you call your beliefs, deep within your cellular structure inside the nucleus where your DNA carries all the codes and information you have long forgotten. How do you unlock this truth? Well, my friends, it is rather simple.

In your meditations, imagine yourself as a tiny point of light deep within your cells, look at your DNA strands and talk to them and they will talk back to you. Your DNA will speak of that truth and much more when you request it. Sometimes, of course, you will have to make conscious your subconscious beliefs before you can change them. To discover how to do that, read on my friends. It is a grand experience that awaits you.

Before you can begin to change your reality as outlined in the previous chapters you have to understand one fundamental truth. An absolute. That truth is:

Your reality is created by the sum total of your beliefs.

Your beliefs form the basis of your reality. Period. Even your feelings are created by your beliefs. Consequently, if there is any part of your life that is not working it is because some sub-conscious belief is limiting you. You may have read about or heard of this concept already. Numerous authors have talked about it. However, it seems that most people do not fully comprehend the extent to which their beliefs can limit them.

One way to get a perspective on the way in which positive or negative beliefs work, is to look at those areas in your life that flow and work for you seemingly without effort. Those are the areas in which your beliefs are in alignment with universal principals and laws. Now, stop and take a look at those areas where you feel stuck and unable to move forward. You will find that you hold beliefs that are out of alignment with those universal principals and laws.

The strongest of all deterrents to growth and awareness are the limiting beliefs that you hold. You will find that it is necessary to work with your belief systems if you are to grow and evolve. You can change or even release and eliminate old ways of thinking and negative belief systems by using the Soul Star and invocation. There is no more effective way to do this.

Beliefs are essentially unconscious, yet they are an integral part of your emotional body and your energies. In order to change them, you must bring them into your conscious awareness.

Most of your beliefs are so deeply entrenched and hidden by fear and ego's resistance to change that they are almost impossible to uncover. There are various techniques that claim to effectively uncover those old beliefs, however they are rarely, if ever, as effective as the Soul Star Mantra and invocation.

The Soul Star Mantra and the invocation process, when applied properly, will expose all of your limiting beliefs and allow you to change them.

Beliefs form the basis of your reality because they attract like energies. When you perceive a belief as **Truth**, you will find circumstances and events that will confirm that belief. By simply holding a belief in your energies it will always attract people, events and circumstances that validate that belief. Consequently, you will find that the events and people in your life will reflect back to you whatever you believe to be true. So, as you grow and evolve, the people that you attract will change. Those who do not share your new beliefs will simply no longer be there.

Most people who choose a higher and more Spiritual path will find that they are constantly recycling their relationships to fit their new beliefs. That is why relationships are so fluid during these times of accelerated evolution and development on this planet.

To give an example; you may be aware of something you want to experience in your life, and yet, however much you wish to bring it into your reality, it remains elusive. You may even begin to form a new belief, but while the old one remains buried you will have much difficulty in actualizing your new belief. You may try to create a new personal Truth, but you will not succeed until you are aware of the belief that is hiding in your subconscious mind.

Some commonly held beliefs are: 'Life is a struggle': 'You have to work hard to get ahead': 'People who have a lot of money are dishonest': 'You can't trust anyone out there': 'Sex is dirty': 'I'm not good enough'.

There are many cultural beliefs which operate in our society that are very pervasive and yet they do not serve us. One example of this is the widely held belief that to receive a reward or money, you have to work hard and struggle. Consequently, more often than not, you find yourself working hard and struggling to get ahead. You can begin to believe that achievement is effortless just as easily. However, most of you do not have that belief.

Or if you do, you only hold it at an intellectual level and you do not embrace it emotionally, as you need to do in order for the new belief to become a reality.

Richard: "Without the mantra and the invocation process I would never have been able to uncover many of the old limiting beliefs that I unconsciously held. In spite of years in psychoanalysis and group therapy, my participation in a six month rebirthing intensive and much more, I still seemed stuck in some areas.

Since discovering and working with the Soul Star and the invocation process I have uncovered many limiting beliefs that I have been able to permanently release and transmute. This has made an enormous difference in my life."

Your judgment and thoughts about others are a good place to begin searching for your limiting beliefs. When you find yourself judging others, look inside and you will find that it is really yourself that you are finding fault with. Those around you merely provide a reflection for *your* issues. When you see their negative or false beliefs, begin to look for corresponding beliefs in your own emotional body.

Sometimes the belief that you are searching for will come up when you are reciting the Mantra; if it doesn't, do the following invocation, or one similar to it. Keep repeating it until the belief surfaces.

If it doesn't come up while repeating the invocation several times over, begin again with the Soul Star Mantra.

This is the invocation:

IN THE NAME AND WISDOM OF SOUL, I INVOKE........... CLARITY AROUND THIS ISSUE AND BELIEF....

To find those limiting beliefs and release them, use this process. Choose an issue or something in your life that is not working for you. You do not even have to be specific, your Soul knows what to bring into your awareness. Hold a focus on that issue in your mind's eye or awareness, enter a meditative state and recite the Soul Star Mantra a number of times until you begin to feel connected to your energies and your Soul.

The Soul Star is an integral part of this process because you need to establish a strong connection to your Soul. You may want to practice with just the Soul Star Mantra several times before attempting this next step.

In order to change your reality you must be prepared to change the beliefs that created it.

At the beginning, as you search for deeply buried beliefs, you may not always experience immediate results. Many of the beliefs you will want to change have been part of your energies for decades, you may even have brought them from other lifetimes. It may not be possible to change a long-standing pattern at the first attempt, you may need to repeat the process several times. Be patient, with practice and dedication you will enhance your skill at breaking down and releasing those old beliefs.

Richard: "I was working with a friend who knew that her purpose in this lifetime included speaking to groups about Spiritual truths and metaphysical issues, yet she was unable to do so. Actualizing her purpose caused her to feel a lot of fear.

While doing the Soul Star Mantra and holding this knowledge in her awareness, she discovered that during many of her lifetimes she had been persecuted for speaking out. She had carried that fear into this lifetime in order to heal it. During the first session, which lasted about forty five minutes, she was able to completely let go of that fear."

Another friend was able to release a block about writing when he discovered a lifetime in which he had been killed before completing a manuscript that he had been working on. Fear came up every time he attempted to write in this lifetime. In the course of this work we have discovered many past life issues that have an effect upon this present lifetime. They are readily released using this simple process."

Changing your beliefs *will* change your reality. This is the most important step you can take to enhance your growth.

You cannot move forward until you have cleared out those old beliefs. It is tempting to overlook the role that your beliefs play in forming your reality. You may feel uncomfortable at first as you search deeply within, for ego can be very clever at avoiding this issue. However, if you are to make the transition from your three dimensional reality to the fourth and fifth dimensions where Ascension can take place, or even if you simply want to make your life work better, it is essential that you look at and work with your limiting beliefs.

The Soul Star Mantra and invocation, used together, are a tremendously growth enhancing process. When you practice the techniques we have outlined with consistency and with dedication you will be rewarded with continuing growth in ways you may never have thought possible.

Chapter Eight Connecting with Your Guides

A Message from Archangel Raphael:

Those of you who wish to know your guides on a more intimate first name basis can do so rather easily. For a very good reason - you have a contract to do so.

This contract was not written on parchment or witnessed by one of your attorneys, it was an agreement you made with those you call your guides before you came into this lifetime. It is something you chose to do when you were not in body, while you were preparing for this incarnation. Why would you want to do this? Because you knew that by choosing to be at the leading edge of the evolution of the planet, you would require a lot of help.

Many of you, as you read and ponder this information will feel a remembrance of that agreement stirring deep within you. Some of you have assignments so unusual and so different that it is imperative you work in concert with your guides during this incarnation. So it is especially important for you to develop a very strong connection to your guides. You will also want to develop your channeling skills in order to bring your guides' message to humanity.

Some of you will channel books and bring new information to the planet in that way. The assignments that others of you have chosen are so unique that it will astound you when the information comes forth. Your guides will help you in many ways, and many of you will be brought gifts of abundance, healing and transformation that will ease your journey.

Ancient knowledge, past and future events are all part of your guide's domain. If it is your path to work intimately with your guide, to bring his message to humanity you will have no trouble doing so, because you would not have been given the task without the innate ability to perform it. Look for your guides signature in your meditations, get to know his particular vibration, for each guide, like each of you, is uniquely different.

You may also call on Raphael to assist you with this endeavor, I will come to you when asked to do so. For instance, I can help you to align with your guide's energy. You are the messengers of the New Age, and we applaud your willingness to play your part in the evolution of yourself and the Earth.

Connecting with your guides, or becoming a channel as it is called is something everyone can learn to do. Channeling is a skill like any other and can be learned by anyone willing to put forth the effort. In fact you are already a channel whether you know it or not.

You are constantly channeling energy through your chakras and other energy systems. Many people channel information from the higher realms without even knowing they are doing so. The crown chakra is the opening through which the channeled information flows into your personal energy system.

Richard: "I was in a seminar in San Francisco, it was there that I had my first channeling experience. A large group of us were learning to be channels. Sometimes people are surprised that channeling is something you can actually be taught to do. It's not always necessary to have instruction, but if you do you will probably learn faster and perfect your skill more easily, especially if you attend a class with a qualified instructor.

Teaching others to channel has become something I love to do. Every class is different and the variety of guides available never fails to amaze me, they are as varied and diverse as the students who come to my classes. Once you decide to become a channel you will attract a guide who has similar interests to you and who will help you to increase your understanding in those areas.

Sometimes a guide may be there just to get you started and then another will come in who is more powerful or may be more aligned with your skills and life purpose. Occasionally, especially in the beginning, a student will channel their Soul or higher self, rather than a guide. When that happens it is always for a very good reason. The time has come in your evolutionary process to form an intimate connection with your own Divinity. Sooner or later everyone should connect with the higher aspects of who they really are."

When it is your intent is to grow Spiritually or be of service to the planet, it will not go unnoticed. The Universe never fails to observe those who are servers of the Light. If you truly desire to work with guides and the higher realms of Light, the Universe will respond.

Becoming a channel for a high level guide is a serious growth step. The guides know the path that you are on and can help you to grow and to learn. Many of them have had lifetimes on this plane, they have experienced the challenges and pitfalls and can help you avoid them. Guidance is available to everyone who is on a Spiritual path. Of course you can choose to make this journey alone, but to do so would be the equivalent of going to a school where there are no teachers.

You are probably receiving guidance at this time whether you know it or not. Becoming a channel will enable the guides to bring you higher quality information and with greater clarity. Like adjusting a radio or TV antenna, learning to channel will help you to make a better connection so that you are able to receive a stronger broadcast from your guide.

The guides and Masters vary as much in their perspective and understanding as we do. The tendency on this dimension, is to assume that there is only one right answer, and that simply is not so. Ask a question and you may get three different answers from three different guides, just as you would get three different answers from people on the Earth plane. Though the answers may vary, the quality and wisdom will be unmistakable. Your own guides will probably have what is for you the best answer.

The guides and Masters have access to the Universal Mind and will often go there for information. They are also interested in efficiency and will readily use the information stored in your memory banks. Channeling for yourself or others, you may be surprised to hear some information you have stored away in your mind and long forgotten being used to solve a current problem. You have much more knowledge and information to draw on than you think you do.

There are many guides available. It is possible to choose the guides you want to work with, however, more often than not the guides will choose you. We recommend that you let the guides do the choosing and the right guide will come to you at the right time.

The guides choose who they want to work with, but not without first consulting your own Soul. Allowing the wisdom of your Soul and the Universe to choose for you is perhaps the best way. There are no mistakes at that level.

Richard: "One day while sitting quietly and beginning to channel, I realized that all my guides had left or at least were not communicating with me. I wondered whether I had done something wrong, why weren't my guides talking to me? After sitting quietly for a little longer, I began to sense a new guide coming in. I felt a very powerful energy presence so I opened to it as best I could. When I asked who it was, the guide responded: 'This is Jesus of Nazareth.'

At first I thought I was making it up, that it was perhaps some trick of my ego or mind trying to make me feel special. I stayed in trance playing with the energy and the connection, trying to decide whether the information was true. I have always been interested in our biblical literature, but I certainly did not expect to become a channel for Jesus, nor had I heard of anyone who had channeled Jesus at that time. The guide continued to reassure me and I finally became convinced of the reality of the experience. It was indeed Jesus. I later found out that there are many who channel Jesus, I simply was not aware of it. My interest in biblical times is probably the result of a previous lifetime working on the development of the Old Testament."

The guides are teachers. If there is something you need to learn or experience, the right guide will be there when you are ready to learn the lesson. As we have said, the guides who come to work with you will often share your interests.

If you are a scientist, you will probably attract a guide with an interest in science. Richard has a friend with an interest in scientific matters who channels Niels Bohr, the deceased atomic scientist. Artistic people will attract guides who will help them with creativity. Similarly, those who do healing will attract guides who work with healing energy. Richard's interest in healing brought Ra-Ta to him, one of the guides who worked with Edgar Cayce.

As a channel you are interpreting a series of impressions. Most channels don't receive a stream of words but rather an energetic impression which requires interpretation. With practice you can learn to do this quite easily. However, if you do not have the vocabulary, you may not be able to act as an interpreter. This is not usually a problem unless the information is highly technical. For example, if you are not a scientist, you may not be able to channel scientific information. If you have ever attempted to translate one language into another you will recognize the difficulty of making an exact interpretation. Given a little practice, you will be able to interpret your guide's message with skill and ease.

Channeling guides can teach you many things. One of the most important is learning to connect and work with the guide's high level energies. These are somewhat subtle and hard to detect initially, but learning to work with them will help you to integrate the higher energies. This will make it much easier for you to work with your Soul and your Light Body, for example.

The more you evolve the more important this becomes. Growth is the result of integrating increasingly higher vibrations of energy into your energy systems. The process of ascension is the transformation of the energies of your cells, your DNA, and the very atoms of your physical body to the very highest frequencies of Light.

Your guide's energies are of a higher and finer vibration than your own. If you are to become a channel you must learn to raise your own frequencies to match those of your guide. Your guide will step down his frequencies as he connects with your energies to facilitate a better connection. This process will **permanently** raise your own energies to a higher vibration and is one of the major advantages of learning to be a channel.

You can also channel your higher self. You are a multidimensional being and you exist on many levels. Aspects of your Soul on those dimensions are every bit as knowledgeable and powerful as any guide. Channeling an aspect of your Soul from the fifth dimension and beyond is as rewarding as channeling guides who are not a part of your higher self.

There are professional channelers who exclusively channel

aspects of their higher selves. All channels at some point should learn to channel their higher selves to gain a better understanding of who they are on other dimensions. Nothing is quite like experiencing your own magnificence and connection to the higher realms.

Richard channels a sixth dimensional aspect of his Soul whom he calls Joseph. Joseph is very popular with Richard's clients and brings a great deal of wisdom to a channeled session. He has told Richard that some time in the not too distant future they will actually merge and become one on this dimension.

Some people who learn to channel will work exclusively with one guide while others will work with two or three. You may also change guides from time to time. Currently Richard is channeling Sananda (Jesus) and Raphael, an Archangel, as well as several others. He has channeled dozens of different guides over the years and always looks forward to meeting new ones.

Many of you who are incarnate at this time are originally of Pleiadian descent. The guides from that dimension are very high level and powerful indeed. Many of them will have *RA* prefixes in their names: Ramtha, Ramarti, Raj-ni, Ra, RA-Sha, Ra-Ta. Because these are usually very high level guides, they may not be able to work with you in the beginning. However this is not always the case.

As you evolve and begin to vibrate at increasingly higher frequencies, you will be able to channel higher level guides or even higher aspects of your guides. In the beginning allow whoever comes to you to work with you, they will be right for you at that time. Be prepared for changes in the guides that work with you as they will increase the richness and depth of your channeling experiences.

One of the most unusual guides Richard has channeled is Hectar. He calls himself a traveler. There was a Star Trek episode about a traveler that seemed to accurately depict who Hectar is. Travelers move about the Universe at will. When Hectar channels through Richard his clairvoyant sight is tremendously enhanced.

Apparently Hectar and others like him occasionally choose a physical body and incarnate for one or more lifetimes. He delights in letting incarnate travelers know who they are.

Hectar is a guide who has a very unusual message. He is very entertaining and he has some thoughts and ideas which are quite controversial. His role is simply to make us think and confront our fixed ideas. One of the most controversial things he says is that he is from a different "God system". He has never clarified what he means by that, but it certainly gets some people stirred up. Perhaps he is what is called a *systems buster*.

He once told a friend of Richard's, an avid reader who also channels, that her intellect was her problem. She immediately rejected that idea, but now admits years later that intellect is not a substitute for understanding. That has been an ongoing theme of Hectar's.

Our intellect can be an impediment to our growth, and often we would be better to try and resolve our problems at deeper intuitive levels.

When you begin to channel a guide you are not familiar with, always ask if the guide is of the Christ Consciousness, or from the Christ Light. If you do not get a definitive 'yes', they are not from the fifth dimension or above. Do not mess around with beings from lower and denser realities than the fifth. If an entity or being gives you any answer other than 'yes', tell them to leave.

No entity can violate that Law. They cannot answer 'yes' if they are not of the Christ light or Christ Consciousness.

This is very important. It is the only mistake you can make in attempting to be a channel.

There are many beings who are not from the fifth dimension or above who would love to play in your energies. Inevitably they are mischievous and do not have your best interests in mind. Recently, it has become more important than ever to verify that your guides are from the Light. The dark forces are feeling threatened as the evolution of this planet increases. They are aware that they are losing ground and are making a more concerted effort to retain control. Much of this is astral level chicanery and you don't want to be part of it. The more adept you become as a channel the less likely you are to be fooled by those lower beings, but nonetheless it is a good idea to validate each guide who wants to work with you.

The love that your guide has for you is one of the first experiences you will have as you begin to channel. That love and compassion will leave you in no doubt as to the reality of your experience. The love that your guide has for you will also help to alleviate any fears that you may have. It is quite normal to have some fear about becoming a channel, particularly in the beginning. You may feel as though you are giving up control when you channel and you may experience some fear around doing that. Personalities usually give up their space rather reluctantly as the ego feels threatened.

There are essentially two kinds of channels, telepathic and energetic. The energy channel brings the energy of the entity into his crown chakra and into his own energy systems. In this type of channeling the entity can speak through the channeler. The telepathic channel simply receives guidance through his telepathic channels and then delivers the message without any help from the guide.

You may also have heard about conscious and unconscious channels. All channels are in trance, some become unconscious and some do not. There is no real difference, one way is not better than the other. Conscious channels maintain a lighter trance and can hear what the guide is saying. Many channels prefer to remain conscious so that they can benefit from the information. Your guide is here to teach you, and the more you hear of what he has to say the more you will learn.

Becoming a telepathic channel is usually a little easier than becoming an energetic channel. The latter is a good way to learn to work with the higher, finer energies of the fifth dimension but to become a telepathic channel is every bit as rewarding as becoming an energetic channel. Often your first experiences will be telepathic. Sometimes, in the early stages you will receive pictures and impressions that you will have to interpret. Your guides know what works for you. You can be assured that whatever unfolds for you is just the right experience.

If you are to become a professional channel you will probably want to be an energetic channel and allow the guide to speak through you. As the energies of evolution have shifted on this planet and raised your energies, it has become easier for the guides to communicate with you.

Meditation for connecting with your Guides

To begin connecting with your guides sit quietly in a meditative state, repeating the Soul Star Mantra to deepen your meditation.

As you do so, call in as much Light as you can into your aura and other energies. Allow the Light you are invoking to carry you higher and higher into the realms of the guides and Masters you are going to connect with.

See yourself taking on the Light and vibration of your guides and Masters. In your meditation imagine your energies going higher and higher calling in more Light as you do so. Find your own energy spiral, whatever that means to you, and add Light to it.

Imagine that your guide is coming closer all the time, perhaps you can see an outline or sense his energy. With each breath your guides is coming closer to you and you are becoming one.

As you go more deeply into your meditation, continue to call in Light. This will raise your vibrations and frequencies to match those of your guides. The guides reside on higher levels and you will need help in integrating their energy with your own energies. They will begin to step down their frequencies to match yours.

Continue the process of mentally raising your

frequencies, using your imagination to help you do so. Any unusual physical responses you feel are probably your guide's way of letting you know that you are connecting with them.

Become aware of your crown chakra at the top of your head. As you become aware of those energies you will begin to experience a conduit opening for your guides to enter into your consciousness. This conduit or channel starts at your crown chakra, goes down behind your eyes, behind your throat chakra and along your spinal column.

With each breath you take, you are bringing more and more of your guide's energies into your body and your own energy systems.

Imagine the energy of your guides entering your crown chakra. There is nothing to do but to allow.

You may feel some resistance to letting your guide occupy your energies as you give up your space to the unknown. Ask him or her if he/she is from the Light. If the answer is yes, just continue to let the Love and Light of this being into your energies and your crown chakra. You do that by allowing and letting go of your resistance.

Breathe out any remaining resistance and let go, allow. Calling in more Light and going higher as you do so.

As the energy moves along your spinal column, you will begin to feel a tension. It is as though there is more of your guide's energy in that channel than it can easily accommodate. More and more of your guide's energy pours down through your crown chakra into that channel that runs down your spinal column.

As the tension builds, suddenly the sides give way, and all of your energies are flooded with the Love and Light of your guide. The energy of your guide moves throughout your aura. You are becoming more and more aware of the presence of your guide's energies within your own.

Ask your guide for his or her name, do not be concerned whether you actually learn it or not. This is an important step. You may not learn your guide's name the first time, but as you play with the energy of your guide's name you are actually making a stronger connection. By repeating this meditation over and over, you will strengthen your connection to your guide. Continue to sense and feel the energy of your guide's name. Each time you do this you will be closer to learning your guide's energetic signature and name.

Begin a dialogue with your guides. You may feel at first as though you are supporting both sides of the dialogue. That you are making it up. That is unlikely, particularly if you have taken the time to go into a meditative state where the guide can more easily communicate with you.

Remember your guides know what works for you. They are tapping into you mind and data banks and are working directly with your Soul. They will assist you with this process. If you feel as though you are becoming confused or are losing the connection call in more Light and speak the word *allow* quietly to yourself.

When you use your imagination and pretend, you are actually helping to strengthen your connection to your guides. Your imagination can be a powerful ally as you learn to work with energy. Much of your reality is created through your own imagination. By simply acknowledging the process and leaving open the possibility that you just might be talking to your guide, you will increase the range and depth of your experience.

If you cannot see or feel your guide at this time, ask your guide to show you a symbol that represents his energy. Each time you do this meditation, hold that symbol in your awareness, add Light to it, and when you sense that you are connected to that symbol energetically, begin a dialogue with it. Perhaps asking what you need to do to strengthen you connection or anything else that seems appropriate at this time.

Treat the experience as though you are a child at play with make-believe friends.

Learning to be a channel can assist you in many ways. There are people who make a living as professional channels, holding workshops and group or individual sessions. Guides can also help you to become more creative in all areas of your life. They can help you become a better writer, painter or musician or help you with the more mundane everyday areas of your life. Of course, one area they always excel at is helping you with your Spiritual growth.

Many healers channel guides who assist them with energy work, body work and with diet and herbal remedies. There are medical doctors who channel guides also, although you are less likely to hear about those.

The guides are great counselors, healers and friends. Their purpose is to be of service to you. During this time of great change and transformation, it can be very comforting to have such wise and loving friends to counsel and console you.

Chapter Nine Creating Your Light Body

A Message from Orin and DaBen:

As the originators of the following information we want to thank Richard for allowing us to bring this information through him. He teaches a somewhat more abbreviated version of the original process of awakening the Light Body.

Times have changed a great deal since we first introduced these teachings to a very select few, of which Richard was one.

The purpose of bringing these processes and teachings to this planet, (they had never before been brought into this dimension or to this planet), was to give you, the student, the opportunity to spiritualize your aura and other energy systems including your DNA.

Previous to bringing these high level energies to your planet it took decades to produce the same result that you can now accomplish in a few short years or less in many cases. This acceleration is in keeping with the accelerated growth of the Earth itself.

As you have learned your planet is quickly becoming fourth dimensional and in order to help you keep up with the growth of the planet many new high level teachings are being brought to you for just this purpose.

This Light Body technology is very important to you

and your planet. Because whether you actively participate in these processes or not you benefit from the increased activity of those who do.

Students who choose to activate their Light Bodies facilitate the growth of Light for the entire planet. They increase the available Light energy for everyone and all benefit from it. They also create a pathway for the energies and the experience, making it easier for those who follow to develop their own Light Bodies.

Make no mistake you will all develop Light Bodies at some point in your evolution, in this life time or some other. It is part of the process of evolution of mankind. Working with energy, especially that of your Light Body, is the fastest growth path available. There is no more effective and quicker method of growth. Some of you have already begun to activate your Light Body on your own.

You can find out about the activation of your own Light Body by going inward in your meditations and asking DaBen or myself to show you what is happening with your own Light Body. If you feel drawn to this information on the Light Body then it is most likely time for you to begin working with these energies. There is no better way to do so than to begin using the Light Body Centers.

Some of you will do this rather easily, others may find it a bit more difficult. You all have guides that can be of assistance to you. There are tapes of meditations put out by the authors and others like Sonaya Roman and Duane Packer who are also grand teachers and who originally brought this work through to the planet and others who also teach these techniques. No matter who you learn from you will find many rewards and much growth available to those of you who have taken this very important step for yourselves and humanity and the Earth.

Nothing is as essential to growth as activating and working with your Light Body.

A fully activated Light Body transforms your physical energy system to higher and higher frequencies of Light. Activating your Light Body is the process that will eventually lead to the Ascension of the physical body.   Ascension, as you know, is the path that the Earth is on. Of course, it is the path that we all are on. The Ascension of the planet is on schedule, but mankind is lagging behind.

If your plan is to ascend in this lifetime there is no better or faster way than activating your Light Body. The process of activating your Light Body is the accelerated path to Ascension. Your Light body can take you there in this lifetime.

Activating your Light Body has become easier in recent years, especially since the anchoring on Earth of the Ninth and Tenth Rays in October of 1992.

Meditation has for centuries been the path to activating your Light Body, and still is, but with the recent planetary changes this process has also changed.   It has been said that it takes one million hours of ordinary meditation to become enlightened and ascend. Is it any wonder there are only a handful of living Masters on the planet today?

Fortunately new ways of activating your Light Body have been developed, and you can now begin to activate your Light Body in just a few short hours.

Your Light Body is multidimensional.

When you activate your Light Body and become more aware

of those frequencies you begin to bring them into this reality. The purpose of all of healing is to make it possible to bring your Light Body into this reality. Most of your Soul's Light and energy resides on other dimensions, but as you begin to work with, and become aware of those multi dimensional energies, you begin to bring that Light into this reality.

The simplest way to begin is to do the Soul Star Mantra in your meditations. By activating your Light Body you create a vehicle for your Soul on this dimension and raise the vibrations of your other energies, even your physical atomic energies.

The Light Body is distinct from your Soul, yet it is your Soul's Light and energy. A concept not easily understood on this dimension where one thing cannot be two things independently.

When you activate your Light Body you bring its Light into this reality and therefore facilitate your Soul's growth in this dimension. Growth is the process of infusing more Light into your energies. As you do this you begin to do two things - raise the frequency of your vibrations, and transmute fear and other issues.

Your Light Body is enormously complex and powerful. It is composed of millions, perhaps billions, of energetic filaments of Light and energy. Under ordinary circumstances, you cannot see them even if you are clairvoyant. You can become aware of your Light Body energy, however, through this new metaphysical technology that has been brought to the planet. That awareness in itself will assist you in bringing more of your Light Body energies into your reality.

We teach students to activate their Light Body by enhancing their awareness of it . This is done in a number of ways and does not necessarily include seeing the actual Light Body.

Using the technology we talk about in this chapter you can become aware of those very high, fine frequencies of Light and energy.

One way to begin developing your awareness of your Light Body is through the sounds of the Light Body Centers. All energy has a corresponding sound, and the Light Body is no exception. The Light Body can be activated by finding the sounds of the Light Body centers and duplicating them verbally in your meditations.

If you are not experienced working with energy or you think you may have trouble finding the sounds of the centers, try listening to the sounds of your chakras. Most of you will have some familiarity with chakras, and this may be an easier place to begin developing the ability to hear the sound that energy makes. Remember to listen with your inner sense not your actual ear.

Finding the sounds of your chakras is a very good way to develop the skill necessary to hear the sounds of the Light Body Centers. It is our experience that finding the tone is the most effective way to help people to access the Light Body Centers. Recently we have found that we have been able to teach people how to activate the Light Body Centers without first learning how to work with the Vibrational Energy Centers.   To simplify this process, we have made recordings of the sounds of the Light Body Centers and their descriptions on audio cassette which you can order from us using the order form at the back of this book.

The Light Body Centers
and
Vibrational Energy Centers

There are three basic Light Body Centers and seven sub centers called Vibrational Energy Centers. None of these centers are chakras, the only similarity is that the sub centers use Earth energy and are similarly placed. The sub centers harmonize and raise the vibration of the emotional and mental bodies.

The Vibrational Energy Centers actually build a bridge between physical reality and the Light Body.   This is the result of the Tenth Ray anchoring the Light Body energies on this planet.

The three basic Light Body Centers are called the Vee, the Fulonia and the SaHa.

In a previous book that Richard co-authored, <u>Creating Your Light Body</u>, he explains how to use the Vibrational Energy Centers and gives more details about the Light Body itself. Refer to the Appendix at the back of this book for further information about the Vibrational Energy Centers.

The Light Body and your Soul's energy are the most transformative energies you can work with. Fear, disease, and other negative energies can readily be transmuted and transformed by that energy. Activating your Light Body and bringing your Soul into this reality is the goal of all Spiritual growth. As you grow spiritually you raise your energies to match those of the higher dimensions where your Soul, the guides, and the Masters reside.

What are the benefits of working with your Light Body? As Richard has continued to activate and work with his Light Body energies, his psychic abilities have increased as has his intuition and ability to access information from other realms and dimensions. He has evolved to the point where his connection to the Universal Mind enables him to bring through new information not otherwise available.

Richard: "Connecting with guides is essentially the ability to work with higher levels of energy. Accessing that connection to your guides and the guidance of your higher self is greatly enhanced by activating your Light Body energies.

Activating my Light Body has led me to many new experiences, one of the most rewarding of which has been my ability to access the higher realms of Light and to channel increasingly higher level guides. I continue to channel many of the same guides, but I am able to reach a higher level of their energy. Some of the Pleiadian guides I have recently met are of such high levels that it is hard to comprehend who they are. My channeling skills are better than ever. This is just one of the many benefits I have encountered in activating my Light Body."

Whether you are a writer, artist, teacher, musician or just want to be more creative in your everyday life, you will benefit from activating your Light Body. Anyone who wishes to be a teacher of metaphysics will find that as they activate their Light Body they will be able to access far higher levels of information and teach from those higher levels.

Your own unique skills and abilities will unfold as you activate your Light Body. This is perhaps one of the most important side effects of activating your Light Body. Your own uniqueness will unfold. For most this is quite an event, because your own special skills, abilities and talents are probably buried under layers of familial and cultural programming. If you are a student looking for a teacher, you would be well advised to look for someone who is actively accessing and working with their Light Body.

Your Light Body energies are some of the finest and subtlest energies you can work with. If you are new to working with energy there are a number of ways to begin, some of which we have already mentioned.

Becoming aware of the energies of your Soul Star is particularly helpful. After working with the Soul Star for a while, try invoking your Light Body energies, using invocation the way we describe in chapter four. You will be able to feel the added intensity that your Light Body energies bring to your efforts.

Remember, you are working with the most advanced techniques available and with the finest and most subtle energies known. So be patient. These techniques will work for you just as they work for us. When we first began to experiment and work with these techniques, it took a lot of practice to perfect our skills.

You become what you focus your awareness on. When you focus on growth and activating your Light Body, you will begin to bring your Light Body to you and grow at unprecedented rates.

Using invocation, you can bring more awareness and more of those energies into your reality. How do you begin to develop an awareness of your Light Body? You can start by meditating on your Soul Star. Continue this for a period of days or weeks, then add invocation.

Allow intuition to be your guide when deciding what invocation to begin with. Choose those invocations that bring you the most awareness or where you feel the greatest intensity.

Like everything in this Universe, the process of creating your Light Body begins with your intent. Your Soul Star is part of this process and is the simplest way to start working with the multidimensional energies of your soul. Your Soul Star could in time actually build your Light Body, but you can greatly speed the process by activating the Light Body using the techniques we describe and by using the three major Light Body Centers.

The Soul Star works first on your physical energies and your cellular energies. In a sense you are working from the inside out with your Soul Star, and from the outside inward with the Light Body energies. There is a definite physical connection with your Soul Star, and therefore we call it an inner connection, but the Light Body energies will reach all levels of your being when you direct them to do so through your intent.

The three Light Body Centers that create and activate your Light Body are the Vee, the SaHa and the Fulonia. The names of the centers correspond to the sounds that they make. To make the sounds verbally, elongate the name of the center as though you were going the sing the word, V-e-e-e-e-e........., S-a-a- a-a—a-H-a-a-a-a, etc.

The Fulonia

You will probably find the Fulonia the easiest to access. The Fulonia is located in the center of your chest about where your heart chakra is. The Fulonia creates a doorway for your Soul's energy to come into your reality and to begin building your Light Body around you.

The Fulonia starts from a tiny point of Light deep within your heart center. It responds via resonance with the sounds that emanate from it and by your awareness of it. In your meditations you may be able to hear the sounds of the Fulonia.

To activate the Fulonia do the Soul Star Mantra until you are in a deep meditative state, then locate that point of Light within your chest just above your heart. This is the first and most critical step. Stay focused in your meditation until you find that tiny oscillating point of Light, then speak the name of the center out loud, remembering to elongate and draw out the sounds of the word Fulonia. As it activates it will expand like a flower coming into bloom.

Remember this is a completely new metaphysical technology; you are one of the first to read about it. Your initial experiences working with your Light Body may not be dramatic and instantaneous but they will unfold as you work with these techniques and energies.

We have already talked about the importance of sound in accessing your Light Body energies. In your meditations, listen for the sounds of your Light Body energies. As you increase your awareness of those sounds you actually begin to activate the centers and create your Light Body as you allow more of those energies into your reality.

The SaHa

The SaHa is in two parts, and is composed of two spheres each about the size of a ping pong ball. One is above your navel and the other below. As you visualize the two spheres in your meditations you can enhance the power of the SaHa by moving them together and then releasing them. Contract the spheres on the Sa and release them on the Ha, elongating the sound as you do so.

By the pumping action created by drawing the centers together and releasing them, the SaHa increases the amplitude and intensity of the energies of your Light Body. It will also intensify your experience of your Soul Star and other energies. You can find the Sa-Ha in your meditations just like the Fulonia, by focusing on the two spheres in your meditations and repeating the sound of the name. It is your intent that leads you to the experience, and even pretending will enhance the experience because your imagination is a powerful creative force. Remember to play with the energies. Do not become too serious and invested in the outcome. Make it fun and with practice you will be able to activate these centers.

The Vee

The Vee Center is located above your head, above your Soul Star and is connected to the ninth chakra, which contains your Light Body energies . It is the most powerful and intense of the Light Body Centers. This center takes the shape of a funnel or "V" when you visualize it and makes the sound of an elongated "V".

When attempting to activate it, picture a "V" shape with the point of the "V" about the center of your chest and the sides of the "V" on either side of your head, speak the name of the center out loud elongating the sound of the "V" for two or three seconds. As it activates some of you may be able to see it as a beautiful flower unfolding. Experiment with the sound by drawing the name out for three or four seconds. As it activates, the sides will come down and the flower will open and disappear, you will either rise up into it or it will come down over you.

If activating your Light Body is your next growth step, you will be attracted to this information and you will want to experiment with the centers. When you begin to work at the high levels accessible through your Light Body you will attract guides and inner teachers who can be very helpful to you. Ask for their help in your meditations, especially when you try to activate your Light Body.

We suggest that you call on a guide known as Aum-een who is one of the Lords of the Light. He has volunteered for this assignment and has been very helpful to us in activating our Light Bodies and developing the Soul Star process. He will come when you call him. Of course there are many others to call upon, they can be very helpful also. In order to obtain their help you must ask for it, that is the rule the guides must follow. Their help must be requested. Of course, sometimes your Soul will request their help and you may be unaware of it.

You have all heard the phrase, *when the student is ready the teacher will appear* (albeit sometimes not in physical form). Help is there for every one on a Spiritual path who requests it.

Some of you will find the Light Body Centers easily, others less so, depending on your ability to sense, perceive and become aware of subtle energies. It doesn't matter how you do that, whether it is sight or sound, feel or any other, but in order to climb the ladder of Initiation you will need to become aware of energy at least in your meditations.

You have the innate ability to do that, because you *are* energy and you come equipped to work with those energies in this (or any other) lifetime. You can choose to evolve and reach the highest levels including those of ascension. Of course, you now know that it has been made easier to do that than ever before.

The opportunity to become a Master, a being of Light on this dimension is a new and unique experiment that you can choose to be part of. You have been given the information and the tools to take your evolution and Spiritual growth into your own hands and shape a new reality.

By bringing your Light Body into this reality you are taking one of, if not the highest, evolutionary steps available.

Your Light Body is who you are on higher dimensions. Instead of having to ascend to these other dimensions you can now bring the energies of ascension quickly and easily to you. You now have the ability to bring the Light of your Christ consciousness into this dimension and reality.

Chapter Ten   Following Spirit without Hesitation

A Message from Sananda

Following Spirit all of the time is of course the ultimate battle of the Spiritual warrior. This is the war between Spirit and personality. Your personality, the outer manifestation of being human, no longer serves you as you enter the higher dimensions.

The Earth has now reached the first division of seven grand divisions of the fourth dimension. It is no longer practical to follow the direction of the outer self, the personality, because it does not know the terrain. This is a completely new experience for your personality/ego. You have incarnated many times, have had hundreds even thousands of lives, yet you are very unprepared for this experience, there are no classes and no schools to prepare you for these uncharted waters. Spirit knows instinctively how to do this but the outer self does not.

It is a grand experiment to take this journey at this time following Spirit wherever it wishes to take you. Many new experiences of joy and wonder await you as you follow Spirit through the twists and turns of this new terrain.

You are never alone. You may feel alone and abandoned as you follow Spirit but that is just your personality's perception. It is reluctant to trust in Spirit. Spirit of course understands this and will gently guide you to those experiences that will begin to build trust.

Your guides are in constant contact with Spirit

assessing your course and helping to make connections along the way. Yes Spirit is a gentle teacher of truth to those who are willing to have even a little faith and trust in their own Divinity. Many of the beings working with you have traveled this road before you and are adding their gentle wisdom to this experience.

Following Spirit without hesitation is the highest Spiritual path you can take. You may follow many paths on your journey and be led to many places, but sooner or later you will come to the realization that nothing is as important as learning to follow Spirit.

Inwardly, you already know that to follow Spirit is the ultimate goal in this and all lifetimes. As you redirect your focus from the outer world to the inner, you will become more aware of this. As Sananda has said, this is the battle of the Spiritual warrior, between personality/ego and Soul. It is a battle that can only be fought from the vantage point of following Spirit.

Think about this for a minute. What would your life look like if every action you took was for your highest good? Because that is what will happen when you begin to follow Spirit without hesitation. Every step and action you take will lead to new growth and learning and will be for your highest good. Your life will take on a new meaning and be filled with the wondrous gifts of Spirit. Instead of responding haphazardly to the messages and direction of Spirit you will be on automatic pilot, constantly being directed to the right place at the right time.

Just the thought of always following Spirit may already be bringing up resistance from the ego aspect of your personality self. Surrendering personal will and giving up ego's wants and desires is a step that everyone on an accelerated growth path has to face at some time, even though it will be greatly opposed by your personality/ego. Not only will Spirit lead you consistently to your highest good, It will always bring to your awareness, the next thing for you to do that will lead to more growth, joy and abundance.

Your Spiritual self is the essence of God individualized. It brings with it to this dimension the qualities of love, compassion and understanding. That energy we call Love is the most fundamental energy of our Universe and indeed all others. It is often said that love is blind, but that is not true of Spirit's love for you. When you are guided by Spirit, every step you take will bring you closer to experiencing yourself as a reflection of God and Love on this dimension.

So what does it mean to follow Spirit? Quite simply, it is to surrender. This is the most important step you can take on your path of personal growth. Once you surrender completely to Spirit, your evolution into higher consciousness will quicken dramatically.

No one surrenders completely, one hundred per cent, all at once. Surrendering and trusting your Spirit more and more will, like anything else, become easier with practice. Spirit, of course, does not need practice. It knows precisely where to lead you and has been waiting for eons for you to take this step.

Certainly everyone can surrender in some ways, but to allow Spirit to become the dominant force in your life isn't always easy. Our culture and society, and most of our institutions are based on fear and control. You have been indoctrinated, from an early age, to believe that almost every facet of your life must be controlled by your personality/ego in some way. The idea that you must be in control of your life and your destiny is widespread and is something that you may not readily relinquish.

Society also tells you what your life should look like and the rules you must follow if you want to be 'successful.' Your Soul's perception may be quite different and Soul may wish to take a path that redefines all of your training and beliefs. When that happens, and it happens for almost everyone on a Spiritual path, your fears will come up. Primarily, fear of the unknown and fear of change. In the ensuing battle between ego and Spirit, ego will try to retain control.

Almost everyone can see the benefits and indeed the necessity for following Spirit, yet giving up control will still be difficult at times. There are many obvious and some less obvious reasons for this. One is that as humans we are primarily driven by our desires for pleasure, comfort and safety, and by the illusion that we are in charge of our lives and our destiny.

Being in resistance gives you the illusion of being in control. By saying *no*, for example, we derive satisfaction by feeling powerful and in control. We obtain pleasure from our resistance. Denial of Spirit is a powerful stance for ego. Egos are addicted to power and control. Giving up that addiction is not easy for ego, even if it is a fabrication and devoid of truth. Our Soul knows that kind of power is not fulfilling, yet because it is known and familiar territory, we succumb to the illusion.

Almost everyone has bought into the illusion of control. You cannot follow Spirit and be 'in control' at the same time. They are directly opposed and you simply cannot do both. Control does not work, it is just more of ego's attachment to old beliefs and programs that can be seen everywhere to continue to fail.

Our response to that failure is always more laws, more regulation and more control. This has gone on for thousands of years and has proved its lack of validity, yet we continue as before. It certainly has not occurred to the majority that you can have loving, fulfilling lives by following Spirit.

When you find yourself in resistance, and it may happen often, it is time to re-surrender. Surrendering may seem like a rather nebulous concept but it isn't. It is actually an energetic pathway that you can become part of by using the invocation below. This pathway is one that all the Masters who have gone before you have taken and made easier to follow by doing so.

Once a pathway is created each person who takes it makes it easier for the next to follow. Try this invocation or a variation of it in your meditations:

> IN THE NAME AND WISDOM OF SOUL, I INVOKE AND ENTER THE PATHWAY OF SURRENDER.

You can use the invocation in your meditations or at any time. Each time you use the invocation and surrender, you increase your ability to surrender. Following Spirit is more than just an ideal, it is a way of living.

We have a set of audio cassette tapes called "The Ascension Series," included is a meditation you can use to find the pathway of surrender.

Following Spirit without hesitation is a skill that you can develop and become more proficient at with practice. You have all chosen difficult lifetimes, and have practiced resistance as a survival mechanism. In fact, your resistance was in the past a valuable ally. It served you well when the infrastructure of society, religious and political organizations, tried to take your power away. If you had not developed any resistance you might have lost your autonomy forever and never have awakened to the Light.

The transformational energies that are here now have diffused much of the power of the politicians and religions, but your resistance, which once served you so well is not something you readily give up. It is time now to let go of your resistance and to surrender to these new energies and to Spirit.

There have been times in your life when you, perhaps unwittingly, followed Spirit's urging and direction. Remember when, without knowing why, you ended up somewhere talking to someone and it turned out they had an important message for you? Or one day, feeling lucky, you followed a hunch and were enriched by the experience. Those are times when you were following Spirit.

Spirit will give more of everything you acknowledge. That is a universal truth. Once you learn to follow Spirit's guidance you will receive more of it. It's that simple.

Following Spirit without hesitation is not just another metaphysical metaphor. It is one of the most fundamental Spiritual principles. The reason is this. In order to grow and to heal you must be in an upward spiral, one that leads to higher ground. That higher ground is always more awareness and higher consciousness. Personality/ego always takes a circular path that leads nowhere. It just goes around and around the same old loop, seeking validation of your old beliefs and programming, even if it never finds it.

As the energies have shifted, especially since the Harmonic Convergence, it has become easier to be aware of the urgings of Spirit.   That is one of the reasons the higher energies have been sent to us. The voice of Spirit is becoming louder and harder to ignore !

A lot of credit is given to left brain analytical thinking in this reality. What the culture sees as wisdom is really just a conglomeration of old truths and behaviors that have never really worked, but might if we put a new spin on them, or so we think.

Logical, analytical thinking without Spirit's participation will not solve any but the simplest of problems, and maybe not even those. Spirit will lead you through the maze of cultural belief systems to whatever is the most fulfilling and rewarding for your growth and personal development.

Whether you are indeed following Spirit or personality/ego is to walk a fine line. There will be times when you think you are following Spirit when in fact you are following your personality's direction   This is one of the most frustrating and confounding experiences that you will have on your path.

Everyone who attempts to follow Spirit faces this dilemma at some time. You are certain you are following Spirit when suddenly, you hit the wall. Things go awry, and you find out that it is your own ego and not Spirit that you have been following. There is always a little trial and error in all new endeavors, and following Spirit is no exception.

So, how do you know when you are following Spirit, not ego? You will feel a profound sense of joy and fulfillment. There will be a sense of ease and being in the flow. Time itself will appear to be greatly condensed because of the efficient way in which you experience it. Spirit will lead you to the very next thing you need to experience with no time wasted. Trial and error will be eliminated. Whatever is for your highest good and personal growth, you will be led to. The increasingly higher energies that are being sent to the planet will assist you greatly with this process.

Following personality/ego is just the opposite. It will be highly inefficient. You will be led down one dead end street after another. Your life will be empty and unfulfilling. You will probably wander from place to place wasting time and missing many opportunities for growth and even abundance.

Like any other process, following Spirit becomes easier when you have done the work involved in connecting you with Spirit. If you have done the Soul Star Mantra hundreds of times (which is not really very much) you will find it easier to follow Spirit than if you were to do the Mantra only a few times. The Mantra and the invocations will deepen your meditations, strengthen your connection to Spirit/Soul and raise the vibrations that make up your physical body. Following Spirit then becomes a lot easier.

As you work with the Soul Star and Invocation, the difference between following personality and following Spirit will become more apparent. In time, you will know absolutely, beyond any doubt, when you are following Spirit and when you are not.

As you begin to follow Spirit, at least initially, there may seem to be a lot of risk involved. For example you may feel a need to change careers, giving up your job to follow an entirely different path, or perhaps leave a relationship or other emotionally charged situation. Take the time to get absolutely clear. One way to do this is to go into meditation.

Do the Soul Star Mantra until you feel very connected, then do the invocation for clarity, as we described earlier in chapter four.

There are tools you can use to assist you in following and connecting with Spirit. The Runes for example, and the I Ching may be powerful tools for you, especially in the beginning when you are just learning to follow Spirit.

Richard: "The Runes are a favorite of mine. I was first introduced to the Runes by a friend. We were sitting in a park one day and I was talking to her about a class I wanted to do. She happened to have her Runes with her and suggested I draw one. The question I asked the Runes was about the class and my inability to find a space for it. I pulled the Rune that has a straight line etched in it. It is the *standstill* Rune. We talked about it and she read me the meaning out of the Rune book.

She suggested she could pull a Rune for me on the same question.

She shook the Rune bag, mixed them thoroughly, and pulled a rune.

It was the same Rune. I put that class on hold and waited for a more auspicious time.

There are many other tools, Tarot, Astrology and others. These tools are a physical representation of Spirit and can be very helpful at times. Do not become too dependent on them, however, because sooner or later they will probably stop working for you.

As you develop your internal listening skills these external tools will no longer be required. This usually happens when your connection to Spirit becomes stronger and you no longer need outside help.

It is time to learn to trust your self and your Spirit. When that happens you will need to go inward for your answers."

Spirit and ego are often in conflict. Ego is infallible at interpreting what you think you want and what you think will make you happy. This conflict between ego and Spirit/Soul is the inner battle you are all fighting. It is the battle of the Spiritual warrior, the polarity of Spirit and matter. This battle wages within everyone who attempts to grow, change and follow Spirit.

Growth often requires that we take a leap of faith. These leaps of faith prompt us to begin to develop senses outside and beyond the limitations of the physical senses. To have faith means to trust your inner knowing and the subtle experiences that awaken you to your Spirituality.

Life in this reality is rarely subtle, and therefore we expect all our experiences to be like the ones we have on this dimension. It simply is not that way in realms of Spirit.

Spirit will place you at just the right time and place to experience what you need. This synchronicity is one of, if not the most powerful forces in your life. You have all experienced so called co-incidence. There is really no such thing as coincidence, what you are experiencing is synchronicity. It is Spirit at work guiding you.

Richard: "A friend of mine became involved in the care of two small children from an abusive home. She couldn't look after them indefinitely, however, she knew of a loving couple who had previously been foster parents. She tried to contact them, but unfortunately the couple had moved and she was unable to find them. One evening she and her husband went to a movie, something they seldom do. You have probably guessed the outcome. The couple she was trying to trace had gone to the same movie. They bumped into one another in the lobby. Not only that, but the couple was considering doing foster care again."

Carol: "The way that Richard and I got together was another of those incredible cases of synchronicity. I had recently moved from Scotland to Seattle, ostensibly to go to school. Things weren't working out quite as I had expected, so I decided to seek some guidance. One Saturday I went to a Psychic Fair, something I had never done before. It was about twenty miles from where I was living at the time. There were fifteen other readers at the fair but when I arrived it was Richard whom I chose to give me a reading. As a result of this meeting we became friends and decided to write together. Later we discovered that we had collaborated on another book many lifetimes ago. That book became the Old Testament. Imagine the complexity of the synchronicity that brought us together again."

Synchronicity is Spirit directed. Like most things involved in following Spirit, all you need to do is acknowledge the synchronicity in you life and you will get more of it. These lifetimes are a journey of self discovery and are a path that you walk alone. At least it seems that way.

When you are on a very accelerated path you may not find a lot of people to walk it with you, or who are willing to keep up the pace. Of course, we are never truly alone, it just seems that way.

Spirit wants to guide you, to walk by your side and take care of you. If you want to be led to those things that will fulfill you and nurture you and that are for your highest good, all you need do is acknowledge the presence of Spirit in your life, and surrender.

Chapter Eleven Detachment

A Message from Bartholomew:

Woe unto those who cannot detach from this reality long enough to reach out and grasp the truth of their existence.

Woe unto those who cannot separate the personality self from the real self, the eternal self. Because if you cannot make the distinction between the illusory self and your Soul you are destined to walk the planes of the third dimension for a long, long time........

And you do not serve your own interests or any one else's by your attachment to the material world.

You have worn out many shoes and callused and blistered your feet for many lifetimes listening to the voice of the material self, it simply no longer serves you to continue that dialogue. You have spoken those words and thought those thoughts that have helped you return here time after time, for as long as you have blistered your feet walking this path of never ending unfulfillment and sorrow.

You have been poet and pauper, pious and blasphemous, martyr and executioner. Are you not ready for something else? Joy perhaps? If not, then hold on to your attachment to this plane and around you will go again.

Do you know that the simple act of detaching from this reality begins the release of your karma ? And if you do not think that releasing your karma is important think about what you have not had in this lifetime. No matter what it is that you would like to have but have not possessed, it is the result of your karmic imprint. Period.

That is quite something is it not? All the suffering, sorrow and bad times in this incarnation. You chose the results of your karma.. Believe it or not, you chose it, your own imprint, with the help of your guides, your own karma. So make it easy on yourself, let go, surrender, detach and you will never see that karma again, it will simply be resolved as quickly as you want it to be.

Perhaps this seems too simple an idea for you, but it is only your attachments that keep you stuck in the third dimension. The one called Sananda, a close friend, says you have been released from your karmic burdens, if you choose to be, and you can evolve as fast as you desire to.

If you are going to continue with your Spiritual growth, sooner or later you will have to learn to detach from those ideas, concepts, beliefs, habits and thoughts that bind you to the material world. Letting go of your attachments and addictions to who you think you are is a very powerful position of growth and evolution. Detachment, surrender and letting go are all essential to your growth, Spiritual and otherwise.

The bad news is that all of your conditioning since infancy tells you otherwise. You have been taught to take a firm grip on your reality and to hold on to all of your cherished dreams and ideas.

Initially, detaching is a somewhat mental process, you use your will and intent in order to detach. Once you begin it becomes progressively easier, you learn to detach by detaching, and as you grow your Soul will assist you in this process.

Not only do we tend to form strong attachments but we become addicted to them. We begin to identify with them in such a way that we **become** our attachments. Your picture of reality is a window that encompasses all the things that you are attached to and who you think you are in this lifetime.

Think about how you identify yourself as a doctor, a painter, or a writer etc. You have probably had thousands of lives on this planet, yet your self image is wrapped around your attachments at this particular time and what you do. Generally, once an attachment is formed it becomes stronger and stronger as you identify more and more with it to the point of habituation. All of these views are of course myopic. You are much more than your personality, what you do and what you are attached to.

Perhaps even more troublesome than your attachments to things are your attachments to your emotional body and its contents; your fear, anger, beliefs and the drama you call your life. Not only are you addicted to who you think you are, but a great deal of who you think you are is defined by your emotional body.

If you don't think this is true, ask yourself when you feel most alive. Isn't it during those times of conflict and intense emotions, when you are warring with your spouse or partner, your boss or someone else? Or when you are 'in love'. Isn't that when you feel most alive? How else could it be when your experiences define your reality and most of your experiences are defined by your emotional body.

There is a paradox here. Most of the time you suppress the contents of your emotional body, but in the heat of an argument you take the cork out of the bottle, so to speak, and let your emotions run. Because you are venting on someone else it is quite likely that you will damage your relationship, so you find out just how harmful it can be to let go of your emotions. So you suppress your emotions and feelings until the next time you have the need to feel your aliveness again.

If you have buried your emotions to the point where you can

no longer release them consciously or are very afraid to express them under any conditions, you will probably identify strongly with your logical mind . Maybe you even define yourself by your thought processes and become the left brain analytical type.

Then of course you become very attached to the picture of yourself as a mental person, even though that is not who you are. It is just where you are parking your identity for now. Not only that, but it allows you to hide from your emotions and feelings. You feel justified in hiding from them because, if you do not, you will identify yourself as *being* those emotions.

We define ourselves in many other ways as well. By the things we acquire, cars, boats, size of your bank account etc. Many women define themselves by their families - especially their children. (Not that we would denigrate motherhood. To bear children holds a special place in all cultures).

If you are a mother, your attachment to your children is probably very strong. Of course, you have a very important role to play in their lives, but they are really not your children, they are God's children. They are Souls on a journey. You are a character in the rich and varied drama of their chosen life experience. The more you are able to view them without attachment, to see them as independent Souls and allow them to become who they really are, the easier their journey (and yours) will be.

Men often define themselves by adopting a material stance such as breadwinner, provider, or head of the family. Or they may identify themselves with their sexual prowess, real or imagined.

So how do you learn to detach? The trick is to begin to view the pictures of who you think you are and the role you are to play as though it isn't really you. They are after all, in the grand scheme, just fleeting images on the material landscape, always ebbing and flowing and giving way to the grander picture of your life as a Soul on a journey through time.

When you are able to detach, you begin to allow that grand design to unfold in this lifetime. But you must be vigilant because some attachments can block your evolution for a very long time. You may have to transcend some very strong attachments if you are to evolve. In the beginning you will need to use your will and your intent in order to detach. When you are able to become the observer, the witness self, you create an opening for growth.

As Souls we have come to witness, not to become ensconced and embroiled in the drama we call our lives. The Soul is intelligent enough to learn by filtering out the real from the unreal and letting go of what does not make sense. We distort this process and dive into fear and other polarities only to become involved in the karmic aspects of the third dimension. We begin to spend lifetime after lifetime balancing karma when all Soul wanted to do was observe and witness this dimension.

The law of cause and effect (karma) is one of the absolutes we experience in this Universe, but it is not something we are compelled to do, it is the result of the choices we make.

We are here to observe and to witness. Anything else is just more attachment to the way things seem to be. The reason we become involved is through ego. When you buy into the belief that we are here to learn lessons, you step into the realm of cause and effect. Your future becomes the past projected forward.

With the recent changes in planetary energies you no longer have to play out your karma. You can simply release and detach from it. How do you do that? There are many ways and we have discussed a number of them. Any technique you use which raises the vibrations of your energies and infuses you with more of your Soul's energy will be of great help.

Ego is the epitome of attachment and defines itself by its experiences, what it calls life on this planet. Ego is especially attached to the illusion that life is finite and ends with the death of the physical body. This is perhaps the most limiting and sinister of all attachments - our attachment to the body itself.

The body is just an anchor, a point of focus, which enables Soul to learn about this dimension. The path Soul is on may include learning and experiencing something over several lifetimes, but because we cannot let go of the ego/body's view of a finite existence we hold on frantically to try to complete those goals in this lifetime. Many people are so attached to the physical body that they hold on to physical life way beyond their time to leave this plane, even when the body is wasting away.

The moment you begin to detach from all your old issues, fears, outmoded beliefs, suffering and other attachments, the easier your life will become. Suffering is not a reality, it is man's invention. Every experience you have that creates suffering in your life, with perhaps the exception of physical pain, is man's invention. Man invented suffering through ego's attachment to the issues and the things in your life.

You are not your ego, unless you choose to believe otherwise. Ego has no intrinsic power or ability to do anything other than defend its turf, which it does rather well. All of your creativity and the other positive qualities and experiences in your life are brought to you by Soul. Most of you are strongly attached to the illusion that you are in control of your life. Man cannot really control, he can only interfere. The Universe always has the last move.

When you trust in the Universe and your Divine plan, everything else becomes meaningless. By giving up control and allowing, you are on the fastest possible track for your evolution and growth.

This reality is no more real than one of Shakespeare's plays, but when you are playing the part it seems very real. All good actors invest heavily in creating the illusion of reality. As you learn to detach and let go, you begin to find your *real* power, the power of the "now", the moment. Soul emerges during those times of witness, of being in the moment.

In the past we have learned through pain and suffering and conflict. This has always been the way humanity learned on this dimension, but it is a limited view. The Law of One states categorically that you are God, you are the creator. God learns through love not through suffering. You are a co-creator with

God.   God can only recreate Himself. It is not possible for the Source to create anything less than Source.

How do you actualize and experience your God self?

Detach. Let go of the perception that you are ego and live in the now, from moment to moment, and you will experience only your Soul's unlimitedness and creativity.

I can hear you say: that is all well and good, I tried it and it didn't work. Ego is very tricky and wherever it sees the opportunity to re-attach, it will. In the beginning you will constantly be falling off the wagon and getting back on, but each time you let go it becomes easier to detach.

If through some revelation or realization you could just detach and never re-attach, you would reach the highest levels of initiation and perhaps even ascend within a few short months. That is how powerful detaching can be.

Sooner or later you will give up your ego's wants and desires and exchange them for a life of fulfillment. As the planet has evolved since the Harmonic Convergence, the greater picture has begun to emerge. That picture has sparked within many a knowing of their greater reality. A sense of their own **I Am** presence, if you will, and it has become easier to integrate concepts like detachment and surrender.

It is still up to you. You choose, you have irrevocable free-will in all these matters. You choose your own path.

We are living in a time of expanded consciousness, unprecedented on this planet. As you work with these new energies and follow the techniques we have discussed in this book, or indeed any other high level growth plan, you will be propelled into higher states of consciousness and awareness than you could ever have imagined a few years ago.

You have two choices. You can live as the illusory, limited self, or you can detach and partake of life on a grand scale. A scale so large, unlimited and plentiful that the mind begins to boggle when you contemplate just how unlimited you can be.

Chapter Twelve The Ascension

A Message from Archangel Raphael:

T he veils were drawn, the darkness had descended, it was cold and bleak, but suddenly - just before the darkest hour - a crack appeared. Light streamed in and began to illuminate the surroundings.

That crack appeared in August 1987, during the Harmonic Convergence. Unknown to humankind, prior to that point in time the people on this planet had very little hope of ever seeing the Light again.

Darkness was all around; the energies of the masses, the mass thought forms were of self annihilation and the stage was set for another catastrophe such as the fall of Atlantis.

There are many versions of what happened, of just what brought about the change, and what kind of energy began arriving on that fateful two-day period of August 16th and 17th, 1987. The clarion call came from much higher realms as the Souls en masse invoked the help of the Source.

Most agree that the Harmonic Convergence signaled a new beginning for the people on this planet; at least for those Initiates and others with the willingness and foresight to take advantage of these magnificent energies.

Humanity's path is to ascend. The ability to become the highest vibration of Light is even encoded in your DNA. It is your birthright to become that being of Light and vibration of Love.

There are many ways to become a being of Light. For example: by activating your Soul Star, using invocation, and by igniting your Light Body or however else you choose.

You have struggled for eons with your limitations in the density of this third dimensional planet. Knowing, though not perhaps in every lifetime that you could indeed someday evolve into the Light of higher consciousness. That is if only you could muster the courage to set aside all of your earthly attachments.

But alas in those other lifetimes your limited self, your personality won every time, so that you had to wait for yet another incarnation. In other lifetimes, you looked upon the stars in the night sky and wondered about your existence here.

Why was it that you always felt there had to be more to life than suffering and struggle, war and famine? Your inner knowing was speaking to you of something greater that you would someday awaken to. Even as a prehistoric man you felt as though the stars were trying to speak to you. They touched something deep within, an inner sense, yet you could not quite interpret what they were trying to tell you. You had not yet gained the consciousness to do that. So you waited patiently for a time when you could know what the stars were saying to you.

Always you looked to the night sky because as you did so you saw a reflection of your own Light, your own inner spark. After many lifetimes, perhaps hundreds or even thousands, your consciousness began to expand as a result of a determined effort to learn a little more with each incarnation. Of course, you were not aware of that gradual expansion with each new lifetime. A slow and gradual, yet relentless evolution occurring life after life. For many Souls life on the third dimension was almost too much. Some of you had to take a break between lifetimes on this planet. Some of you may have been here rather infrequently like Richard, but nevertheless you came back.

This planet is a beautiful place, addictive even, in spite of the density of the energies. It is one of the few places where all the colors of the rainbow actually exist. It is also one of the few places where there is a waiting list to come aboard. Beings are lining up to be here because of the new opportunities to take part in the first phase of the physical ascension of the planet and its inhabitants. The Earth is known throughout the cosmos as a planet of suffering, yet the competition to be here is intense.

For those who master this dimension the rest of existence is really rather easy. The brave Souls who have come here at this time know why they have chosen to be here. You knew that you were in for the ride of your life, so to speak. You knew that in order to make a difference you were going to be challenged and confronted like never before.

Mankind is at a crossroads. The door has been opened for those who wish to evolve, but many more are oblivious to the changing realities of life on planet Earth. There is no call to arms on the nightly news or the afternoon talk shows.

The masses are asleep. They simply refuse to heed the call of the Universe to wake up. Even those who are waking, who are beginning to hear the many messengers, are slow to heed another truth: that the planet is on a collision course with its own destiny and that course could spell the end of mankind as you know it. You have been listening to the wrong messengers on this planet. You have given your power away, you have given it to the churches, the politicians, the corporations and in other ways too many to mention.

You have given it away in mass for the promise of a better life. That so called better life has brought you many things; cars, homes, RV's, boats etc. But at what price?

You no longer know who you are, you live in fear behind locked doors afraid of the darkness that begins to descend around you. The children in the streets are crying out, who am I, why do I feel so much pain, why do I not know who I am?

The decay of the cities is not a coincidence. It is the result of giving your power away, of giving up your right to choose and your right to your Divine uniqueness. Becoming instead one of the gray masses who do not have one single clue as to who they are and where they are going and whose desire for security overrides everything. Most people believe their security is in the hands of the corporate managers and bosses or the police, politicians and other authorities.

Wake up my friends. You control your destiny, you are autonomous. You are Hu-man, God man, yes that's what human means - God man. If you meditate, ask in your meditations to be shown what it means to be Hu-man. If you do not meditate on a regular basis, how in the world do you think you will evolve? By watching TV or reading more of those books on how to be Spiritual?

No matter how good the books, they are mostly entertainment. They will perhaps give you some insight into who you are but you must take that into your meditations if you are to heal and change enough to unlock your God-self.

Listen also for the God sounds in your meditations. The sound of the Hu at the highest levels. You can ride that sound into many dimensions, it will also awaken you to your true self.

Very few have passed through the doors of Initiation who have not made meditation a part of their daily lives. When Jesus said (or more accurately Maitreya speaking through Jesus) 'I am the way', he was not talking about becoming a Christian. He was speaking of the fact that it is **He** who guards the door of the first two Initiations on this planet (of which there are twelve in total). Each Initiation up to the fourth means that you are merging more and more with your essence, your Soul. The Soul merge begins at the third level and culminates at the fourth where you begin to connect to even higher levels of your Oversoul and Monad.

The process of Initiation was in the past long and arduous, and took many lifetimes to accomplish. The recent massive shifts of energy coming to the planet mean that it is now possible to merge with your Soul and reach the level of the sixth Initiation, or even higher in this lifetime. You can probably do so in a decade or perhaps less, but it will not happen without strong desire and intent. It is not something you can do in your sleep.

Actually because of the new energies some of this work does go on in your sleep but it will still be of no avail unless you become a conscious co-creator of your own Divine plan for this lifetime.

The Ascension of this planet will occur on schedule and if you are to be part of it and survive you have work to do to regain your power and to actualize your God self. Your brothers and sisters, aunts and uncles may not be getting the message but obviously you are. At least intellectually, but that is just the beginning. It is not your job to awaken the masses or even your own family, so you can stop running around telling them about the wonderful revelations you have had and the wonderful information you have acquired in all of those books you have read.

Look in the mirror my friend, your reflection tells you many things including that you are a marvelous, magnificent co-creator who has probably forgotten who he is. It is time to become earnestly involved, to do the work, to merge with your Soul.

Due to recent energy shifts it has been made infinitely easier to receive the gift of Divine Love and to awaken to your part in the Divine plan, to actualize your God self. You have free will, you can choose to awaken or not. But if you choose not to, be aware that your judgment about others, their ignorance and denial of their all powerful, all knowing God self are projections of your own self judgment. It is only through your own growth, your own healing and expansion that you can help them. It is up to you to do the inner work.

Richard: "About a decade ago, out of inner knowing or desperation I decided I had had enough. I was going to heal this lifetime and make my life work better. Within days of the decision, I met a lady who was doing what she called rebirthing.

Subsequently I was told loud and clear by my higher self, to begin rebirthing. I had begun channeling about a year prior to this. Becoming a channel was actually the first big step, however I didn't know that at the time.

The things I know and write about now, I knew little of

prior to the Harmonic Convergence. My experience did include a background in things psychological and I was aware of psychic phenomena and was beginning to become aware of some psychic ability. But that was all. So, seven years ago I was a babe in the woods not having much background or knowledge of things Spiritual or what it really meant to heal a lifetime.

Like all of you, I was receiving guidance from the Universe and, of course, I had done some of this work in other lifetimes, however I did not know that at the time. Unknowingly I was beginning where I had left off in another lifetime. My intuition tells me that I came into this lifetime slightly above the first level of Initiation. That is the point where you first begin to be influenced by your Soul.

Every lifetime has the capacity to reach very high levels of Initiation, so whether you are an Initiate or not at this time isn't really important. If you are curious about this, write to us and one of my guides will tell me what level you are on and I will write back and let you know.

Initiation is really about the integration of your own Soul into your energies. The result of Initiation is that you become more and more aligned with your Soul and your Divine plan for this lifetime. You also become Soul directed instead of ego directed.

Another thing that happens at the Soul merge or third Initiation is that your third eye, also known as the sixth chakra, opens and you become more intuitive. Many become very psychic, in fact all of you will become psychic at that level if you simply allow yourself to.

Perhaps the most significant change in my life is that I no longer feel separate. I have healed that place of feeling alone and separate from myself, my God and the planet. I spend a lot of time alone, I am single, not in a relationship and at the time of writing am perfectly content. Of course, someone will probably appear in my life in the near future to help me heal more of my relationship issues.

Fear is just about non existent in my life, I still have a little residual anger from time to time, but when I began to heal and do rebirthing I discovered I was a living volcano of rage from a very abusive childhood. Much of that abuse is now healed. The most significant part of healing my abuse issues is that it has changed the dynamics of my relationships. If that was all that I could achieve from the work that I have done that would be enough.

As I recognize and acknowledge my Spirituality I have begun to heal and integrate on a much larger scale, multidimensionally. My oneness with God, the Source, the all that is."

So, now we come to what Ascension means to you. As we stated earlier, Ascension is so much a part of the Divine plan for humanity that the ability to ascend is encoded in your DNA.

Actually it is the ability to create a Light Body that is encoded in your DNA. That means that your body is the path to Ascension.

The concept of Ascension is not new. Many individuals have been able to ascend to the ranks of Masters during the course of recorded history and even before that. Some retained their physical body and remained on the planet, others did not. It is our understanding that the first to ascend from this planet was Maitreya in Atlantis. He has now reached the level of the seventh Initiation and embodies the Christ consciousness for this planet.

For those of you who are not familiar with the story of Jesus and Maitreya, we will cover it briefly. Jesus of Nazareth was a Third Degree Initiate when he began his mission and teachings.

As a Third Degree Initiate he could not have accomplished all the things attributed to him. Of course, that was known at a cosmic level and so was his mission. In order to compensate for that, Jesus was overshadowed by Maitreya, at the time a Sixth Degree Initiate. In a sense Jesus became a channel for Maitreya. He was not strictly a channel as we know it today. Overshadowing was much more consistent and complete. The overshadowing by Maitreya occurred during the last three years of Jesus' mission.

Jesus received the fourth level of Initiation at the time of the crucifixion and is now working as a Sixth Degree Initiate. Jesus is now in charge of the world's religions and will soon be overshadowing the priest who is to become the new Pope.

Needless to say, the world's religions need a lot of work. Their teachings are not now and probably have never been in touch with the plan for the Earth. If you have not heard about this before and want to know more, it is covered more completely in the <u>Mahatma</u> books by Brian Grattan.

The Ascension referred to in this book, is the same process that all the Masters who have ascended have accomplished, however, there are a few important exceptions.

One difference is that it has not been possible to Spiritualize the human body before to the point where the actual physical body, including all of its organs, could be dematerialized and rematerialized at will. We are rapidly approaching the time when this will become a real possibility.

Another difference is that it took countless hours of meditation to reach Ascension. Some who previously ascended spent as much as twenty hours per day for forty years to ascend. If you are already an Initiate you can reach those high levels of Initiation in less than a decade, perhaps spending less than an hour per day.

Essentially, Ascension occurs when your energies reach frequencies higher than the highest on Earth. The highest frequency on Earth today is the seventh level of the astral plane. You would have to reach the sixth level of Initiation at a physical level to ascend the body.

This evolutionary step is imminent, and once someone does it, a pathway will be created for all who wish to follow.

Exactly what it will take for you to reach your highest potential must be determined by you, your Soul and your guides. Your Higher Self or Soul will tell you in your meditations what it will take for you to ascend.

If you are thinking that all of this is confusing and you do not know how or if it applies to you, you can bet that is just more of your ego's resistance to change and doing the necessary work in facing your false beliefs, old programs and fears. We say this because, as we have stated you are programmed and coded to accomplish Ascension in this lifetime or indeed any lifetime.

At inner levels you know how to accomplish Ascension. However it has become a lot easier for you now. So you really do not have an excuse do you? Your three dimensional personality is probably saying, "So I'll do it if the rewards are adequate for the investment of my time and effort."

Well, my friends, you are going to have to trust a little here. You are going to have to listen to your Soul and your inner knowing and Soul probably won't send you a registered letter. You will simply have to learn to trust, which is probably a major lesson in itself. Trust and faith do not come easily to most , but trust and faith in the Universe are the mark of the Spiritual warrior and something you will have learn more about as you take this journey.

Know this if you do not already. You are eternal now, but your body is not. If you die before you have Spiritualized your body, you will have to start all over in yet another body, that is if you decide to come back to the planet. You will shed much of your ego and personality at the fourth level of Initiation. This will vary somewhat from individual to individual.

In the past the Fourth Initiation spelled the death of the physical body. That is no longer the case. Initiations have become much more subtle and easier to deal with, however the personality/ ego still puts up a lot of resistance.

For the first time on this planet, as of 1992, there has been a coming together of all the energies needed on Earth to enable man to Spiritualize his physical body so that he could ascend with it. Until recently it has not been possible to Spiritualize the matter of the physical body to the point where it could be ascended. The energies that have recently come to the planet include the Ninth, Tenth, Eleventh and Twelfth Rays. An important aspect of those energies was the anchoring of the 9th and 10th Rays which activate your Light Body. These rays complete the anchoring of the energies of the Source, your I AM Presence on this planet. They are very powerful transformative energies, and are the highest level energies available at this time.

The teachings in this book are designed to take you to the Third Initiation, the Soul merge and beyond, perhaps to the Fifth or even the Sixth. All of the energy techniques we teach will accelerate your growth tremendously regardless of the level you are on or whether or not you are an Initiate.

Becoming Soul infused greatly raises your consciousness and facilitates your connection with your higher mind so that you have a greater understanding of your life here on Earth and your place in the Divine plan for mankind . You will simply become more integrated and understanding of humanity and yourself. It doesn't matter whether you resonate with this information about Ascension or not. If you want to heal your life and change your reality you can, it's up to you, it's the same process.

Once you reach Ascension you will become a channel for Divine Will and have everything you need without effort to carry out your own unique purpose in the Divine plan. If your plan encompasses having a palatial mansion and a large bank account you will have it, but be on notice, part of your plan may be to live on a remote island without any modern conveniences.

You will love every minute of your existence no matter how it looks. You will be able to materialize and dematerialize and travel from place to place at will. Some of you will choose to go elsewhere. You will be able to bi-locate, be in two places at one time if you wish. You will be surrounded by loving compassionate beings all the time. If that's what you want.

This journey may take some hard work and some sacrifice but so do other rewards that pale by comparison. It will not always be pleasant as you work through your old issues, programs and fears. You may be inclined at times to want to give up. You cannot put this journey off for ever. In this lifetime or another, sooner or later you will take a stand. We think your time is **now**.

Appendix

The Vibrational Energy Body Centers

In this appendix we describe in detail the seven Vibrational Energy Body Centers. (They are not chakras.) Their primary function is to control and set up the energies of the emotional and mental bodies. They organize and harmonize the energies we take in and receive from our environment and from the people we encounter.

The knowledge of the Vibrational Energy Centers and the Light Body Centers is new. Information about them is being gathered as we use them and teach about them. We know that they process and harmonize energy and enable the human aura to take on a finer vibration and a spiritual shimmer.

As we learn about these Vibrational Energy Centers, we realize that not only are they are not chakras, but their function goes beyond what the chakras do. As we learn to work with them and prove their existence to ourselves, we can explore these centers, study them, and perhaps write about them. We will each come to our experiences from our own inner work and personal point of view. Therefore, our experiences of these centers are unique for each individual.

We cannot emphasize enough that you need to have an almost playful attitude when working with the Vibrational Energy Centers as well as the patience to observe and sense. You must learn to recognize the feel of the frequencies as they move through the centers. Allow your intuitive abilities to read the energy, sense it, and become aware of the shifts and changes.

The Vibrational Energy Body Centers use earth energy. This is the type of energy that humans and all things of the earth are made of. Our personal energies, including those in our aura, are composed of and use earth energy.

There are very fine, high vibration earth energies that normally we are unfamiliar with and cannot ordinarily incorporate into our energy systems. As we begin to use the Vibrational Energy Body Centers we gain skill at working with those finer frequencies. We begin to set the stage and build a base for using the higher and finer energies of the Light Body Centers.

You should learn about and work with the Vibrational Energy Centers before you actually begin the process of activating the Light Body Centers. Harmony and balance is needed in the emotional and mental bodies to enable you to work with the higher and finer light that will build the Light Body. The Vibrational Energy Centers are an integral part of building and using the Light Body but they are also very versatile and are used for a multitude of purposes.

We are composed of earth energy and the Vibrational Energy Centers use the earth energy. They can be used for healing, easing pain, and transmuting the distorted energy patterns of others. The Centers are used to hold a space for others to heal physically and emotionally as well as to heal oneself. To use the centers for self healing, all one has to do is run the energies and concentrate their awareness on the area you want to heal. Perhaps, the only limitations to the use of the Vibrational Energy Centers is one's imagination.

The frequencies of these energies can be used to transcend space and time. We have used them in class settings where we have traveled to other dimensions. We have used them to help make our connections with the High Self or Soul, and we have used them to channel extraterrestrials. Especially the Vibrational Energy Centers can be used in meditations to reach very deep states.

The list of uses for these centers is long. Using the energies will allow you to expand your consciousness, increase your awareness, and assist in problem solving by enhancing your intuitive powers.

In addition to setting a foundation for the Light Body Centers, perhaps the most important use of these centers is to untangle the emotional and mental bodies and restore the feeling of oneness and harmony in our lives, the world, and universe in which we live.

It is possible, working with the Vibrational Energy Centers, to loosen the trapped feelings of old wounds and long forgotten trauma. But these feelings can also be transmuted quickly by using and running the energies. It has certainly been our experience that growth and healing take place at an accelerated rate using these centers.

Important to the personal discovery and use of the Vibrational Energy Centers is the sounds that the centers make. Little has been written about the capabilities of sound, but it is important because all energies have corresponding sound frequencies that can be used to connect you with the energy. Listening with your inner ear for the sounds of the centers as well as being aware of any other energy pattern will facilitate your connection to them.

We have noted that the Vibrational Energy Centers are not chakras; however, as an exercise to show yourself how energies emit sound frequencies, try listening for the sound of your chakras. Chakras are a little more fundamental and therefore more easily heard. The sounds associated with them are quite easy to discover.

Of course, of primary importance is the fact that the Vibrational Energy Centers lead us to the experiences of the Light Body Centers and the radiance they bring. The Vibrational Energy Centers take in energy from the area surrounding an individual, process it, and harmonize it for the use of the emotional and mental bodies.

Nu'a

The first of the Vibrational Energy Centers is called the Nu'a (pronounced Nooya) and is located for women just inside the vaginal wall. It is activated by a small muscle near the front. Do not contract the complete pelvic floor, as this can cause irritation to the bladder. In men the Nu'a is located slightly in front of and above the prostate gland. Experiment a little until you are able to begin to isolate the muscle. A gentle easy contraction is all that is necessary. The first two of the lower Vibrational Energy Centers can be activated in our consciousness by these muscles. The Nu'a draws energy from around us and begins the harmonizing process of that energy to enable us to make use of it.

The Nu'a is cone shaped. The smallest part or the top of the cone is located approximately at the area of the prostate gland in men and at a similar location in women. The bottom of the cone is located closest to the earth.

The cone can be opened or closed at will once you learn to work with the energies. It can also be raised or lowered. The amount of energy brought into the Nu'a cone is regulated by this opening and closing or raising and lowering.

The name of each of the Vibrational Energy Centers and the Light Body Centers is also its sound frequency. Saying the name is used to assist in the center's activation.

The Nu'a as the first of the Vibrational Energy Centers begins the process of moving the energy upwards through the other centers.

Dinia

The second center is the Dinia which is in the form of two rather elliptical spheres, located on each side of center in the lower abdomen. These spheres are activated by saying their name (din-i-a) and contracting muscles located in the area just below the navel. The Dinia make a pulsing movement when they are activated. They, in a sense, flatten and inflate as they take the energy from the Nu'a, process it, harmonize it, and send it outward in waves and upward toward the other centers. As the energy moves outward from the Dinia, it forms a plane that moves out from the body that can be raised or lowered to regulate the amount and kind of energy that you take in or release. Observing and following this plane of energy as far out as you can is an excellent exercise in learning to recognize and sense these energy frequencies.

These two lower centers, the Nu'a and the Dinia, are the first of the centers that harmonize and stabilize the energy in the emotional auric field, also called the emotional body.

The Nu'a and the Dinia can be influenced consciously in several different ways. It is encouraged that you play with these methods of working with the Nu'a and the Dinia to find that method which will best enhance your experience and awareness of the energy frequencies involved. When repeating the names of the Nu'a and Dinia, play with changing the cadence of the syllables. For example: *Noo-ya* or *nooo-ya* or with the Dinia; *din-din-i-a* or *dinnn-i-a or din-iya* and so on. This is sometimes easier followed while listening to guided meditations, but there is no reason you cannot play with it.

The same can be said for playing with the Nu'a cone or the Dinia plane. Use your imagination and visualization to work with lengthening the Nu'a cone and changing the angle of the cone as it moves out from the body. The cone can be lengthened almost to the shape of a tube.

Generally the energy moves out from the Dinia spheres in a horizontal wave, out as far as your consciousness can follow. But this can be influenced also by using your imagination and visualization to raise and lower the angle of this plane of energy.

Be advised that extending the cone of the Nu'a and increasing the angle of the Dinia plane can bring a great deal of energy into your system. If you are running your energies in a place where the energy is not harmonized, you may wish to keep the angles lower to prevent taking too much of the distorted energy into your system.

Leow

The third of the Vibrational Energy Centers is located approximately in the area of the abdomen just below the solar plexus. It is called the Leow (pronounced Lee-ow). It is a spherical center that is made up of three smaller spheres that when activated move around themselves while each rotates individually. This double rotation moves into a second stage when the three spheres reach such speeds and random rotations that one is no longer able to consciously follow their movement. It is then as though the Leow bursts into a ball of brilliant light.

The Leow gathers the energy that is moving upward through the Nu'a and the Dinia and processes it on upward.

Mumin

Just above the Leow is an energy membrane called the mumin. When the Leow is activated the energy moving upward causes the mumin to form a dome. We can consciously influence the type of energy frequency that is allowed through the mumin. We only need think "the mumin is transparent to all lifting frequencies," or harmonizing frequencies, and so on.

The mumin is not a Vibrational Energy Center itself, but acts as a filter to the frequencies moving up from the Nu'a, Dinia, and Leow.

Ranthia

Above the mumin is the fourth of the Vibrational Energy Centers called the Ranthia. The Ranthia can best be described as a more or less spherical shape. From a center axis, it is divided into four membranous divisions much like a revolving door.

The movement of the Ranthia cannot be influenced consciously but only observed. Often the depth of your experience with the Ranthia depends on your ability to allow and observe.

The Ranthia acts as a regulator of the energies as they move up to the upper centers. As the intensity of the energy moving up from the lower centers increases, the divisions (the revolving door-like membranes) of the Ranthia will billow out much like the sail of a boat as it fills with wind. As the intensity decreases the divisions tighten up. In this way the energy moving to the upper centers remains steady. The activated Ranthia revolves but is unpredictable in the speed and direction of its revolutions. This may change while the energies are being run or may be different each time they are run.

The four lower centers, the Nu'a, Dinia, Leow, and the Ranthia when activated, process and harmonize the energy in the physical and emotional bodies. There is indication that these centers will assist in healing the physical body and will harmonize and balance the chakra system. There are many aspects to healing the physical body. All of these must be taken into consideration such as the reason for the disease, the thoughts that have created it, how well we are caring for our body, and so on. But to use the Vibrational Energy Centers to assist and affect a healing, one need only run the energies and hold the area of the body in need of healing in the conscious awareness.

The processing of energy through the lower Vibrational Energy Centers tends to set up the emotional body, allowing emotions to come to the surface and be dealt with. It allows emotions to come and then go so that we do not hold on to them. This process in itself is very healing because we tend to hold on to our emotions, instead of allowing them to flow and be released.

The upper Vibrational Energy Centers work much the same way for the mental body as the lower centers work for the emotional body. As the energy that is coming up from the lower centers passes through the upper centers, it sets up our thoughts and assists in clear thinking and the release of thoughts as they move through the mind and the mental body.

Traeo

The fifth Vibrational Energy Center is called the Traeo (Tray-e-oh). It is a band around the throat area with energy extensions out from it much like feathers, petals, or leaves. As the energy moves upward from the Ranthia, the Traeo focuses the energy and sets it up for the next center the Pieah. As the energy moves upward the "feathers" lift and wave out from the band. The Traeo is another center that is not affected consciously but simply observed.

The experiences of the Traeo can be quite varied with reports of the "feathers" appearing long or short, or sometimes more like iridescent waves of energy. Some see them as leaves. Generally, the Traeo band is on a plane that is not quite horizontal. At times the "feathers" can extend almost vertical from the band due to the energy moving upward through them.

Pieah

The next center, the Pieah (pie-e-ah) is a sphere located inside the head, behind the eyes, close to the pineal gland. It basically has two functions. An individual can center their consciousness inside the Pieah. By doing this they essentially enter a void that silences the thought process. The second function takes place when the Pieah is activated. As the energy from the lower centers moves up to the Pieah, multiple light rods pass through this center. They work to set up and clarify the thoughts as they arrive and move through the mental body. The activated Pieah allows us to think more complete thoughts with an amazing clarity.

We can learn to fully develop our thought process and let go of and even extinguish thought that we do not want to hold onto. This can be a wonderful process for helping us recognize and rid ourselves of limiting and old thoughts that no longer serve us. As the thoughts move through the mental body, and as the processed and harmonized energy moves up through the Pieah, the rods extend out, move back and forth, and for all practical purposes, light up. They have something of their own rhythm in this process.

Renawre

The last of the Upper Vibrational Energy Centers is the Renawre (re-naw-re). It is a horizontal band located above the head. The refined energy moving up from the other centers moves through the center of the Renawre, in a last refinement through the Vibrational Energy Centers. This highly refined energy cascades out over the Renawre and down around the physical body for a cocoon-like gridwork of fine energy around the body. The Renawre, as well as the Pieah, cannot be affected by conscious thought. Again, one simply observes.

When you begin working with the Renawre it may not be possible to observe the cocoon of energy all the way down to your feet. But as you continue to work with the centers, explore the frequencies of the Renawre, and continue to harmonize their energies, you will be able to observe the cocoon enclosing your entire body.

Two of the centers seem to be dominant and are used perhaps more than the others. These two centers are the Ranthia and the Renawre. The Renawre is the overall regulator of the energies of the center and seems to be closely tied to the energies of the aura. The spiritual shimmer that eventually develops in us from working to activate our Light Body appears first in the Renawre and then the aura. The Ranthia, perhaps because of its location at the heart area, is also a major center. Its functions have to do with sensing energy, as well as working with soul and the energy of Love. Many of us have shut down the heart area out of emotional pain. We are, therefore, limiting our capacity to love and be loved.

Even though the Vibrational Energy Body Centers are not chakras, in many cases they are located very close to them. The chakras that are located close to the Vibrational Energy Centers will benefit from, and can be regulated and harmonized by, running the energies and using the Centers. The energy of the chakras will be balanced, cleared, and more organized because the finer energy will transmute the lower energy of the chakras.

The energy of the Vibrational Energy Centers is very definite and can be felt on a physical level. This is one way to gauge what is going on as you work with the Vibrational Energy Centers, because this physical connection will grow.

It may be necessary for some, or even most of the readers to find a teacher who can help them learn to find and activate the Vibrational Energy Centers and the Light Body Centers. It is always a good idea to work with a teacher and others who have already begun the activation of their centers, simply for confirmation and verification of what you are doing.

Both authors, even after being involved in the process for quite some time, still continue to have doubts about the process. At times of ego resurgence, we wonder if it is working for us or if it is our imagination. These are questions that will come up for you also. It is ego's way of trying to maintain the status quo in the third dimension.

The kinds of profound experiences you can have when beginning to activate the Light Body can be almost mind blowing to our third dimensional way of thinking. For all these reasons it is advisable to have a teacher and a support group with whom you can discuss the process. Sharing the profound experiences can help you learn to recognize the blocks that your ego will place in your way. Support can help you through the times when your fears and life issues come up and you must face them.

Creating your Light Body, as a road once started, is difficult to leave. But at times it may also be difficult to go onward as well. This is simply because you are healing your life and so much of what needs to be healed has been with you for a long time. We are not only healing this lifetime but all the issues brought into this one that have not been healed in other lifetimes. This can be quite a process.

For those who wish to try to work with the Vibrational Energy Centers and the Light Body Centers on their own (or at least try to find them and study them) we recommend this process:

Assume a position of comfort, preferably sitting in a chair where you can keep your back relatively straight. It seems to be helpful to some to lower their right leg slightly. These positions do not seem to be too crucial because both authors are a little different in their approach to meditation.

Allow yourself to close your eyes and begin to go quietly inward. Start at the lower center and use your intuitive abilities to get a sense of the Nu'a cone. Richard uses an inner knowing of the position, feel, look, and sound of the Nu'a and the other centers. He does this to locate and help activate them. Carol uses a visualization technique to gain a sense of the centers.

Because the Nu'a and the Dinia are both activated by muscle contraction, again use your inner sense to find the muscles that activate the Nu'a and Dinia. Practice selecting the muscle; use your sense of knowing. Ask for guidance.

Once you have a sense of the center and are ready to begin to work with it, say its name, Noo ya. Start with a regular sound, simply breaking up the syllables. Later you can experiment by holding the sounds, drawing them out, etc. Contract the muscle on the Nu and release on the Ya.

Once you get a sense that you are able to activate the Nu'a, move on to the Dinia. Do the remainder of the centers the same way, remembering that the first two are the only two that are consciously activated by muscle contraction.

The Leow through the Renawre cannot be consciously influenced, but are activated by saying their names, again breaking them down into syllables. Once they are activated, learn to observe.

While running the energy of the .Vibrational Energy Centers, you may simply feel a sense of movement, floating, or perhaps a feeling of emotion. What you are feeling is the movement of the energy, and the activation that is taking place.

If you feel discomfort in any way, adjust your posture slightly. You may find it helpful to bow your head slightly to open your neck area. This will allow any excess energy to be released. If you feel like shifting, do so. If you cannot rid yourself of discomfort, move back to the center just prior to the one that you were working on that brought about the discomfort.

The Light Body Centers are activated in much the same way. But a great deal of harmony and flow is needed in both the emotional and mental bodies for the successful activation of the Light Body Centers. Work with the Vibrational Energy Centers a great deal before starting with the Light Body Centers. In fact, work with each center until you are comfortable with what you are doing before you add the next center.

Begin your work with the centers in the meditative state for three to four times a week for ten to twenty minutes. Increase the time if you feel comfortable with what you are doing.

Channeled Phone Readings
with Richard Dupuis

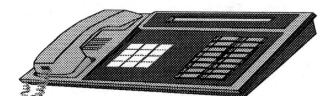

Call 1-800-480-6021
and
Talk with the Ascended Masters & Archangels

- ♦ **Raphael** ♦ **Ashtar**
- ♦ **Sananda** ♦ **Sanat Kumara**

or any of the other Ascended Masters
and Archangels Richard channels.

A Channeled Reading with the Masters will
help you:

- ♦ Solve personal problems.
- ♦ Increase your abundance.
- ♦ Heal your life.
- ♦ Enhance your growth.
- ♦ Find and explore your life purpose.
- ♦ Improve the quality of your life.

Your inquiries and questions will be answered with
Love, Compassion, and Wisdom.

Richard Dupuis
Meditations and Courses
on Cassette

Summary of Meditations and Courses
For a complete description and listing, use the Request for Information Form at the back of this book. To order, see the Order Form.

1. Activating Your Soul Star
A *powerful* 30 minute meditation to *remove your blocks to growth.*
.... 9.95

2. The Ascension Series
Two hours of meditations including:
Activating Your *Soul Star*   Merging with Your *Soul*
Working with the *Energies of Ascension*
Invoking Your *Light Body Energies*
Building a Pyramid of Light Around You
.... 29.95

3. Beginning Your Journey to Mastery
Two hours of meditations:
Attaining the *Third Initiation*
Anchoring Your *Soul Star* in Your Physical Body
Opening Your *Heart Center*   Unifying Your *Chakras*
Meeting and Working with *Sanat Kumara*
Preparing for *Higher Initiations*
.... 29.95

4. Creating Your Light Body
A *complete course* on *activating your Light Body* with eight 30 minute meditations.
Letting Go of Resistance to Change
Building the *Rainbow Bridge*
Invoking Your **I AM** Presence
Working with the *Mahatma Energies*
Accessing and Activating the *Light Body Centers*
Discovering Your Life Purpose.
Exploring the *Consciousness of the Electron*
Working with Your DNA.
Invoking the Energy of Your *Oversoul*
Increasing Your Awareness of Your *Source Star*   59.95

Order Form for Books and Tapes
by Richard Dupuis

TAPES	PRICE / EACH		QTY	$ AMOUNT
	U. S.	CANADA		
1. Activating Your Soul Star	9.95	12.95		
2. The Ascension Series	29.95	38.95		
3. Beginning Your Journey to Mastery	29.95	38.95		
4. Creating Your Light Body	59.95	77.95		
BOOKS				
Ancient Wisdom	10.95	13.95		

*Sales Tax Information
Residents of the following locations, please add the sales tax indicated: Canada 7.0%

CA 7.5%	MA 5.0%	PA 6.0%
CO 3.0%	NC 6.0%	TX 8.25%
CT 6.0%	NJ 6.0%	VA 4.5%
GA 6.0%	NM 6.5%	WA 8.2%
IL 6.25%	NY 7.0%	WI 5.5%
IN 5.0%	NYC 8.25%	
KY 6.0%	OH 6.0%	

SUBTOTAL	
*SALES TAX	
**SHIPPING & HANDLING	
TOTAL	$

**Shipping and Handling Charges

Orders up to $15.00	$2.50	$35.01 to $50.00	6.25
$15.01 to $25.00	3..50	$50.01 to $75.00	8.00
$25.01 to $35.00	4.50	Over $75.00	9.75

SHIP TO: NAME

STREET ADDRESS

CITY   STATE   ZIP

Your Phone Number (In case we need to call you about your order.)   HOME PHONE   WORK PHONE

Make checks payable to: Council of Light
300 Queen Anne Avenue North, No. 613
Seattle, WA 98109-4599
Telephone (206) 781-2418

Tear Here

Tear Here

Request for Information

YOUR NAME

STREET ADDRESS

CITY | STATE | ZIP

Your Phone Number (In case we need to call you about your request) | HOME PHONE | WORK PHONE

☐ **Please send me a FREE copy of your NEWSLETTER and a CATALOG of TAPES and SEMINARS.**

☐ **Please send me a SCHEDULE of CLASSES and WORKSHOPS you will be holding in MY AREA.**

I am interested in attending the Classes checkmarked below:

☐ Creating Your Light Body

☐ Channeling (Connecting with your guides and High Self)

☐ Spiritual Growth - Working with your Soul Star and other energy systems

☐ Manifesting with Light - Creating your life the way you want it

☐ Developing Your Psychic Abilities

☐ Releasing Blocks to Growth - Working with issues of fear

☐ Healing with Energy & Light

☐ Introduction to Meditation

I am interested in SPONSORING one or more of your CLASSES:

Questions or Comments

To receive the information you have requested, send this form to:

Council of Light
300 Queen Anne Avenue North, No. 613
Seattle, WA 98109-4599
Telephone (206) 781-2418

Tear Here

Tear Here

Request for Information

YOUR NAME

STREET ADDRESS

CITY		STATE	ZIP

Your Phone Number (In case we need to call you about your request)	HOME PHONE	WORK PHONE

	Please send me a FREE copy of your NEWSLETTER and a CATALOG of TAPES and SEMINARS.
	Please send me a SCHEDULE of CLASSES and WORKSHOPS you will be holding in MY AREA.

I am interested in attending the Classes checkmarked below:

	Creating Your Light Body
	Channeling (Connecting with your guides and High Self)
	Spiritual Growth - Working with your Soul Star and other energy systems
	Manifesting with Light - Creating your life the way you want it
	Developing Your Psychic Abilities
	Releasing Blocks to Growth - Working with issues of fear
	Healing with Energy & Light
	Introduction to Meditation

	I am interested in SPONSORING one or more of your CLASSES:

Questions or Comments

To receive the information you have requested, send this form to:

Council of Light
300 Queen Anne Avenue North, No. 613
Seattle, WA 98109-4599
Telephone (206) 781-2418

Tear Here — Tear Here — Tear Here

Order Form for Books and Tapes
by Richard Dupuis

TAPES	PRICE / EACH		QTY	$ AMOUNT
	U. S.	CANADA		
1. Activating Your Soul Star	9.95	12.95		
2. The Ascension Series	29.95	38.95		
3. Beginning Your Journey to Mastery	29.95	38.95		
4. Creating Your Light Body	59.95	77.95		
BOOKS				
Ancient Wisdom	10.95	13.95		

*Sales Tax Information
Residents of the following locations, please add the sales tax indicated: Canada 7.0%

CA 7.5%	MA 5.0%	PA 6.0%
CO 3.0%	NC 6.0%	TX 8.25%
CT 6.0%	NJ 6.0%	VA 4.5%
GA 6.0%	NM 6.5%	WA 8.2%
IL 6.25%	NY 7.0%	WI 5.5%
IN 5.0%	NYC 8.25%	
KY 6.0%	OH 6.0%	

SUBTOTAL	
*SALES TAX	
**SHIPPING & HANDLING	
TOTAL	$

**Shipping and Handling Charges

Orders up to $15.00	$2.50	$35.01 to $50.00	6.25
$15.01 to $25.00	3..50	$50.01 to $75.00	8.00
$25.01 to $35.00	4.50	Over $75.00	9.75

SHIP TO: NAME

STREET ADDRESS

CITY   STATE   ZIP

Your Phone Number (In case we need to call you about your order.)	HOME PHONE	WORK PHONE

Make checks payable to: Council of Light
300 Queen Anne Avenue North, No. 613
Seattle, WA 98109-4599
Telephone (206) 781-2418

Tear Here · Tear Here